ON THAT DAY
A TRILOGY

ON THAT DAY

Thomas Fitzhugh Sheets

ReadersMagnet, LLC

TABLE OF CONTENTS

PROLOGUE

A word of welcome and a word of warning. In the first chapter of Galatians, Paul warns us of a gospel, other than the one he preached, that would lead to eternal condemnation. In this book you will find an emphasis on how God's saving grace, plus a genuine faith and works of service combine to save (Ref. Eph. 2:8-10, we are not saved by works, but we are not saved without them - James, "Faith without works is dead"). When you truly make Jesus Christ Lord of your life, day-by-day, you need not worry about salvation - salvation takes care of itself. If you have allowed someone to put salvation in your rear view mirror - you will find that for those first disciples, salvation was in their windshield. "Faith is being sure of what is hoped for..." (Hebrews 11:1).

In John 1:12, John changes the landscape of The Promised Land from a land of entitlement to a land of opportunity. "Yet to all who received him, to those who believed in his name, he gave the right to become children of God-".

In John 2, Jesus performs His first miracle - turning water into wine at a wedding banquet (party) and foreshadows the celebration that happens when He returns for His Bride, The Church.

In John 3:3-18, Jesus gives Nicodemus a new vision of entering His Eternal Kingdom and pairs inclusion and exclusion - based on belief. Unbelievers are condemned this side of the grave.

In John 4:23, Jesus says "...the true worshipers will worship the Father in spirit and in truth, for they are the kind of worshipers the Father seeks.".

In John 5:28-29, Jesus echos Daniel 12:1-3, when He will call all those in the grave to rise to be judged, to be included in - or excluded from, His Eternal Kingdom. "...-those who have done good will rise to live, and those who have done evil will rise to be condemned." Note: Those who do not believe have already been condemned. Here, Jesus condemns the many who call Him Lord and then calls them - evildoers. (Ref. Matt. 7:21-23)

In John 6:27-29, Jesus tells his disciples, "The work of God is this, to believe..." and then He makes it very hard for them to believe. All except the twelve desert Him never to return. Then Peter identifies Jesus as the Messiah, the one sent by God to fulfill The Promise God made to Abraham, (verses 68-69). "Simon Peter answered him, 'Lord, to whom shall we go? You have the words of eternal life. We believe and know that you are the Holy One of God.' "

In John 8:30-44, Jesus shows how hard it is for the children of Abraham to believe and put their faith in Him. Because of this, they became the children of the devil.

Peter captures the story of this journey from new birth to salvation in 1Peter 1:3-5, "Praise be to the God and Father of our Lord Jesus Christ! In his great mercy he has given us new birth into a living hope through the resurrection of Jesus Christ from the dead, and into an inheritance that can never perish, spoil or fade - kept in heaven for you, who through faith are shielded by God's power until the coming of the salvation that is ready to be revealed in the last time." The pivotal phrase here is "who through faith" which makes this a faith journey - a faith which he quickly describes as a genuine faith.

Let's look at 2 Timothy 4:7-8 for Paul's story of him completing his faith journey. "I have fought the good fight, and I have finished the race, I have kept the faith. Now there is in store for me the crown of righteousness, which the Lord, the righteous judge, will award to me on that day (Day) - and not only me, but also to all who have longed for his appearing." Here Paul reveals the driving force in his faith journey and by extension ours - the faith of The First Century Church and the faith that saves (justifies). Paul connects his and our "blood, sweat and tears" to The Blessed Hope of our reward - eternal life at Christ's Second Coming. These are qualities we hold in common with other citizens of the Kingdom. Its like he is building that small gate and narrow road to the Kingdom for those who look forward to His appearing as the Righteous Judge and thus the awarding of that citizenship to those who belong - having those same qualities.

These passages above from The Gospel of John show how hard it was for Jesus to change the landscape of The Promised Land - the land of entitlement into the land of opportunity for all people. This parallels the American Experiment - of people coming to a new world and it becoming the land of opportunity. In this book you will find, in part, the story of that American Dream being shattered by those who would return us to a land of entitlement.

What is going on in America today is a spiritual war between the godlessness of a socialist dream of utopia (Marxism) and God's promise of paradise made to a thief as he and Jesus died on a cross. Pushing back against that darkness is a never ending war that must be in our spiritual DNA because Satan never gives up - The Gospel of Jesus Christ vs the gospel of Big Brother.

This book is a continuation of my first effort, "The Road to Restoration". As I continued to write, God led me to an understanding of Paul's convertion that made this whole project worthwhile. As a Pharisee, Paul came to his encounter with the risen Christ with a saved mind-set that was sacred to him as it was to all Pharisees. Years later, Paul writes in Romans and Galatians about being a child of the promise of salvation. His conversion was therefore from believing he was saved, possessing salvation, to that moment of reward, resurrection and the fulfillment of the promise God made to Abraham - at Christ's Second Coming.

I never had a sense of having been saved, so it was easy for me to see myself, like Paul, living in the light of the hope and promise of salvation. It was also easy for me to see the people around me, with their sacred saved mind-set, being in the same darkness Paul was in before his encounter with Christ. This is the convertion that most in our culture desperately need to have today. Living in the light of the promise of salvation rather than the in darkness of the possession of salvation. Paul details his conversion very vividly in Titus 3:3-7 (read NIV). He also tells us that this is the foundation of his faith in Titus 1:2 (NIV prior to 2011).

I hope as you read you will see how this evolved in my head as I did not know the end from the beginning. I did not work from an outline and only wrote as I was being led by the Spirit.

FOREWORD

The Death of THE PROMISE

"Searching for the Keys to the Kingdom Finding
Three Days of Grace"

The white-knuckle grip of an 11-year-old boy held the old
Church pew in front of him so that he could hardly remain
standing as the Church congregation droned out yet another verse
of "Just As I Am". The Preacher was sopped in sweat for a full 40
minutes as he preached a strong message of "once saved, always
saved" and with shouting admonitions—lured and lulled those
hearing and fanning congregants towards the belief that if ONLY
they would profess Jesus, "walk down that aisle" and agree to be
baptized, they would be once and forever saved from hell and
made fit for heaven.

That young, anguished boy, "walked the aisle" that night and
soon received a "dunking" in a nearby creek and that's all there
was… except he was expected to attend Sunday School for the
rest of his life, read his King James Version Bible and count on a
most certain delivery into eternal Paradise whenever he should die.

But is this the whole truth and nothing but the truth? Within a few years, this boy, who is now reflecting on nearly 50 years of "Church life" harmonizes with the Author of this beautiful book a resounding "NO." In the swamps of Church conflict, in the dark nights of the soul – looking for the elusive abundant life in the eyes of others and failing to see that spark of Divine – a fuller, more inclusive theology comes into view which asks, along with Thomas Sheets "Is Salvation an event or a process?"

The kindling of such a bonfire question may begin with two simple verses and hopefully, will blaze within you unto a raging fire of living by faith, leaning deeply into grace as a full time "kingdom builder" in view of these words:

> *For the message of the cross is foolishness to those who are perishing, but to us who are being saved it is the power of God. 1 Cor 1:18 NKJV*

> *For we are to God the fragrance of Christ among those who are being saved and among those who are perishing. 2 Cor 2:15-16 NKJV*

This very day, so many of our Evangelical Seminaries continue to create "cookie-cutter heretics" who become the newly ordained Leaders of our Churches and who preach a perilous, heretical doctrine of "certain and eternal salvation," which is poor and haughty theology. The Holy Spirit, through my friend Tom, has ripped apart this paint by numbers canvas of cheap grace and putrid theology, and for this, may we all be grateful. Therefore, Tom will take no credit for these insights. I believe this author is a mystic in the tailored favor of unsung prophets of this current age. Publishing books today costs lots of money for most authors and when one is inspired by the Holy Spirit to write, and when words are dictated through the flow of rapid-fire keyboarding happens to "an uneducated Theologian" (Tom's words) then we all have a case of consideration to challenge the putrid and rotting theology of some of our Sunday morning sermons.

You might want to put on your boots. As you read forward, the "budding staff of Aaron" just may come into your grip. This staff is a fit tool for a new Reformation of bold Christian proclamation. The death of "once saved, always saved" as an altar event is before you to yield a brightness for this dark age that the winter of our souls has long-awaited.

W. Lee Eames Jr. Summer, 2019

W. Lee Eames Jr. served as a Baptist Pastor for 25 years, as an Airport Chaplain for the North American Mission Board. He holds a Masters of Divinity Degree from Southern Seminary and Counseling Credentials through the International Society of Neurolinguistics and Neurosemantics.

INTRODUCTION

Reaching for the Brass Ring

Perhaps you are familiar with the brass ring that you could reach out to the old carousels. If you grabbed that brass ring, you were rewarded with a free second carousel ride.

The brass ring in the Christian faith is eternal life. When people are taught that at the moment of belief they possess eternal life, they will stop reaching for that brass ring.

While writing, I came to believe the brass ring should also represent a restored relationship with God. Because of their disobedience, Adam and Eve were kicked out of paradise, and this broken relationship between God and mankind must be made right before anyone may "eat from the tree of life and live forever."

To suggest that belief and some wise and persuasive rhetoric will gain you the keys to the kingdom seems most inadequate. The only remedy for disobedience is obedience as a means to restore that relationship. This should be the brass ring that we continually reach for in our faith journey.

Belief in Jesus as God's son is step one in the journey, but to suggest that eternal life is the next step and that all righteousness follows from that is not supported by God's Word. Scripture supports a childlike faith in God. This childlike faith that Jesus demands of us is not out of fear of death, but only a devoted, loving, joyful obedience to the Father. Walking with God in this loving parent-child relationship is what gives hope to those who have made Jesus Lord of their life—the hope of receiving a rich welcome into the kingdom of God.

The Bible is the revelation of God's plan to restore the relationship with mankind that was lost in The Garden of Eden. Eternal life is promised, but it is only reached by a journey that focuses on this restored relationship. "Seek ye first the kingdom of God and His righteousness" (Matthew 6:33) speaks to this dual purpose. Any attempt to make salvation achievable without including the righteousness that God requires of us is a distortion of Scripture.

The journey that leads us to this restored relationship has many milestones on it: God's promises to Abraham; Jesus, the fulfillment of those promises; and the Holy Spirit as promised by Jesus. Each prompts us to desire a right relationship with God the Father. These are the most important milestones to me, and they also make my understanding of God's plan of restoration the most important milestone on my journey.

As I journeyed, each of these milestones—and more—seemed like steps that completed the journey, only to be led to the next step. Looking back, it seems that I was trying to find out why I saw my salvation in my windshield while most people around me saw their salvation in their rearview mirror. I did not have the saved mindset of so many of my friends. At its extreme, some of them let me know that without that saved mindset, I could not be a Christian. I was living in the promise of salvation while they lived in the possession of salvation.

The journey after conversion could be defined as a spiritual civil war that breaks out inside each of us. Paul defines this as a war between our flesh and the Holy Spirit that is now living inside of us. Before conversion, we are lord over our own lives. After conversion, the Spirit and the Word lead us to make Jesus Lord of one's life. "He restores my soul, He guides me in paths of righteousness for His name's sake" (Psalm 23:3) best defines in a few words the sacred journey from conversion to salvation.

MARKETING A UTOPIAN MYTH

I spent many hours talking with my pastor in an attempt to reconcile what he believed and taught with what I was beginning to understand concerning Jesus's Second Coming. My understanding and focus on Christ's Second Coming was the prevailing view in early American churches.

Advent churches held on to that view as the culture began to move away from that focus. Around 1840, advent churches began to appear in response to this change with the most notable and visible being the Seventh-Day Adventist Church. Also, on a smaller scale, The Advent Christian Church, which I attended for two years, came into existence in response to this drifting away from the focus on Jesus' Second Coming, moving toward making salvation an entitlement after conversion.

I chose to join the Adventist movement after reading an article by Dr. Lee E. Baker about The Advent Christian Church. In the article, he makes a statement that helped me know that I was not alone in my journey. He states, in part, "Man is a candidate for immortality by the grace of God, though not the present possessor of it." With that statement, he put salvation in the windshield of all believers and put to rest for me the debate that has been raging for over 400 years. The debate over eternal security I now find to be foolish. You cannot keep or lose what you do not yet possess.

It's a hope and a promise. It's an inheritance that we cannot claim this side of the grave. "Come, you who are blessed by my Father, take your inheritance, the kingdom prepared for you since the creation of the world" (Matthew 25:34).

Dr. Baker also used the term conditional immortality, which I believe is exactly what set this movement apart from the rest of the Christian culture. I understand this term to mean that my immortality is conditioned on my response to the grace of the cross and promise of life after death. This line of thinking has a lot in common with the contra-Calvin movement of Arminian belief and the early Methodist Church but is rare in today's culture. For example, I believe The United Methodist Church's decline and problems of today are closely related to their movement away from Arminian belief, and thus the debate.

Note: In the late 1500s, Jacobus Arminius disputed Calvin's theology with five points of disagreement. Those who agreed with Calvin came up with the five-point Calvinism (TULIP), and the debate was on. John Wesley was an Arminian believing that Calvin was wrong. While I know that I am loved and chosen by God, I cannot take either of those realities to the extreme of being unconditional. I am neither unconditionally elected into the kingdom nor am I unconditionally loved into the kingdom. These two extremes seem to try to escape judgment as if there is no consequence for being disobedient—both avoiding the conditional commands of grace.

The movement away from this line of thinking is progressive in nature as it tends to make salvation an entitlement at the moment of belief or conversion. Along with this understanding, I was becoming aware of the similarities of this trend in the church and the progressive movement in our government. The progressive movement in our culture, as I understand it, both inside and outside the church, may well be the cause of this drift.

Progressives and socialists, inside and out, are like two peas in a pod, both preaching entitlement. I believe an impatience with God's fulfillment of His promise of restoring us to paradise is at the heart of this progressive, socialist agenda.

Progressivism became more accepted after the Reformation, along with the popular belief that, through the power of government, man could create his paradise or utopia. It is noteworthy that recently an avowed socialist marketing a utopian myth came very close to being nominated by the progressive Democrat Party as their presidential candidate. The progressive culture of today seems to have a lot in common with the Jewish culture that Jesus came into. This is especially true in the area of eternal security and the saved mindset of possessing salvation (ref. John 5:39–40).

At its founding, the culture in America was Christian, and in fact, our first colleges were founded to train clergy. Now, a culture counter to that culture has grown up in America. The church is, to a large extent, no longer a culture counter to that new American Culture. To me, this is sad but true, and to believe the very church is being threatened by the progressives inside the Beltway (the politicians in Washington, D.C.) is to miss the fact that the progressives took over the church with the "believe and be saved" message, which became the focus in the church, particularly after World War II. At the heart of this socialist progressive movement is in giving people a sense of entitlement to anything that someone else has earned. This is also at the heart of teaching someone that, at the moment of conversion, you are eternally secure, entitled to the kingdom.

Progressivism, no matter how or where it's applied, tends to discourage our reaching for the brass ring. The most seductive way to avoid working on restoring this lost relationship is to convince people that paradise is their birthright, thereby making it an entitlement. The Jews did it, and now Christians are doing it. Is it any wonder that so many young people are so enthusiastic about the liberal, socialist, progressive agenda? I believe that the rise of the progressive culture in this country, especially in our universities and government is, by and large, the force behind the decline in Christ's Church in America.

It may well be that what we are doing today is exactly what Adam and Eve did in the Garden in their reaching for the fruit in disobedience. Our knowledge of God has been replaced by the knowledge of good and evil. Until we understand this and work to restore this relationship, we will forever work on our knowledge of good and evil at the expense of our knowledge of God and our relationship with Him. We all live under the curse with the knowledge of good and evil in a world that gives us a taste of paradise. The only hope that we have of returning to paradise is to restore the relationship with God that was lost because of disobedience.

> "The golden rule for understanding spiritually is not intellect, but obedience. If a man wants scientific knowledge, intellectual curiosity is his guide, but if he wants insight into what Jesus Christ teaches, he can only gain it through obedience" (Oswald Chambers, My Utmost for His Highest.").

Since the focus on obedience is seldom, if ever, found in the church, the foundation of the theology of the church today is essentially intellectual curiosity. Without a focus on obedience, it follows that our theology is mostly a product of our knowledge of good and evil. In the pursuit of salvation, belief counts for nothing if it is not followed by a singular focus on being led by the Holy Spirit in devoted obedience to God's Word and making Jesus Lord of one's life.

One element of this culture that I find particularly disturbing is the acceptance of the total depravity of man or the total inability of a man to come to a saving knowledge of Jesus Christ without a divine appointment. The other side of this coin is that some are preordained not to have that divine appointment and are therefore doomed to eternal separation from God. This is very problematic for me in that I believe only an unloving god could be capable of such a thing.

The divine appointment and God saving only the predestined elect seems to work well with the eternal security approach in that "what God has done can't be undone." I have a hard time putting God in that box. Is this a "blame it on God" approach, and is it the only way to get people to believe something so unbelievable? (ref. 2 Peter 3:9.)

This concept was taught, in part, in the 1500s to a culture that was mostly illiterate and ignorant of what was actually in the Bible. This began to be challenged in the late 1500s and 1600s and led to the Methodist movement in the 1700s. Underneath this theology is the belief that man is born in sin, dead in his trespasses, and unable to do anything on his own to come away from that.

Starting with Abraham and Isaac, the blood sacrifice of an animal was done periodically for the atonement of sin so that being born in sin was no longer counted against man. Jesus is the atoning sacrifice, once and for all. Abraham was justified by this blood sacrifice and put his faith in God's promise of life after death (Messiah) and deemed righteous by that faith.

The word regeneration is used to describe the moment of passing from death to life, the moment of salvation. Abraham is still in the grave, and his regeneration moment will be at Jesus' Second Coming as will mine. "While we were yet sinners, Christ died" and "Behold the Lamb of God who takes away the sin of the world" mean what they say. Jesus's work on the cross makes the sinful condition of our birth a nonissue. The issue then becomes how we respond to that gift of grace freely given.

In Luke 9:18 and following, Jesus starts by identifying who He is and that He is going to be killed but fails to mention the manner and significance of his death. The response of doing what He asks is therefore not in gratitude, but an act of obedience and by extension, an act of worship. We are to do this to secure the promise of eternal life, which is a matter of faith and lordship.

I nibble around that response a lot. When Jesus says for us to pick up our cross daily, I think that could be a veiled reference to the grace that we are to offer to our little world—the world around us. Jesus says that we should forgive others as He forgives us in the Lord's Prayer and conditions His forgiveness on how we forgive. That is a monumental demand. If we fail to grasp the magnitude of His grace in paying our debt and fail to forgive in like manner, might the issue of being dead in our trespasses remain and, if so, would we lose completely the benefit of His sacrificial death? This reinforces the idea of conditional immortality I mentioned earlier.

The conversion moment for each person is unique and mysterious, and it is supposed to be that way. This should be left up to God and the individual and should be treated as a sacred moment without prejudice. What is not mysterious is what the new believer is to do after conversion, which is to follow Jesus, a sacred journey that leads to the genuine faith that Peter describes.

In Peter's letters, we find a picture of what faith and discipleship are all about. He tells us what he is looking forward to, how we are to endure hardships, and presents the dynamics of holy living, but with some warnings. Why should Peter be so sure of his salvation yet warn readers not to distort scripture that leads to their destruction and not to is led astray by false teachers and fall from their secure position unless there is a dire consequence for doing so? He lived in anticipation of Jesus' Second Coming and warned that in the last days, scoffers would come and say, "Where is this coming He promised?" (2 Peter 3:4).

Jesus said, "Many will say to me on that day, Lord, Lord, did we not prophesy in your name, and drive out demons and perform many miracles?" Then I will tell them plainly, "I never knew you. Away from me you evildoers!" (Matthew 7:22–23). He follows this up with a therefore and the "wise and foolish builders." "Everyone who hears these words of mine and puts them into practice…every one who hears these words and does not put them into practice" is identifying the foundation of those he has just condemned as the problem. They are guilty of Christian malpractice, and the very foundation of their faith is the problem.

What is the difference between the foundation of those Jesus has just condemned and those who will hear at that moment "well done, thou good and faithful servant"? That last quote is from the parable of the talents in Matthew 25 and is in contrast to the one-talent servant who hears "You wicked, lazy servant…throw that worthless servant outside, into the darkness."

I think it's fair to say that the foundation of the Christian Culture today (with few exceptions) is that, at the moment of belief, we gain heaven and everything that follows is built on that foundation. If Satan's end game is for us to hear on that day "away from me, you evildoers," he must get us started on the wrong foot. We have at least two examples of how Satan operates: first, with the serpent tempting Eve through instant self-gratification by mixing truth with lies; second, when the devil tempts Jesus by mixing truth with lies, he also offers instant self-gratification.

This passage (Matthew 7) is a warning that begins, "Watch out for false prophets as they come to you in sheep's clothing, but inwardly they are ferocious wolves." This sounds to me like Jesus is warning us against those who tell us that, at the moment of conversion, we get the keys to the kingdom, and, at the moment of death, we go to heaven. That's what we want to hear, and also that is the wide gate that precedes this warning. It's an appeal to both our desire for instant self-gratification and our fear of going to hell.

This approach seems to be working, but which road does this mind-set put us on? Easy belief and cheap grace are terms that have been used to describe this approach, but I don't believe they quite capture the absurdity of this mindset and belief. Jesus says follow Me, and it is neither cheap nor easy. He demands self-denial and self-sacrifice from those who choose to follow Him, which is much different than deciding to believe. Jesus connects both to our eternal reward.

SOUNDING THE ALARM

I believe that God has led me to sound the alarm on what Jesus is warning us about at the end of the Sermon on the Mount, and He is tying what happens at the judgment of what happens at the very beginning of this journey at our conversion. Living in an unfulfilled promise of salvation, which is fulfilled at His Second Coming (ref. Hebrews 9:28), is hard enough without adding the self-denial and self-sacrifice that Jesus requires and results in the genuine faith Peter describes. This is not an easy decision but is the decision that a believer must make as he decides whether or not to follow Jesus, along with the devotion that comes with it.

It seems to me that the appeal of instant self-gratification is at the heart of what Jesus is warning us about, and it has tragic consequences if unheeded. Note that Jesus begins His teaching ministry with this warning in the Sermon on the Mount and ends His teaching with a similar warning in the Olivet Discourse in Matthew 24 and 25.

Beliefs are like grains of sand in that, under the microscope, they are all unique and are shaped by every current of air or water. Don't build your faith on the sandbar or dune of belief and let it become the foundation of the foolish builder. Obedience is the main ingredient that turns the sand of belief into the mortar used to build the rock-solid foundation of faith for which the wise builder is commended. We are saved by grace through faith, which begins with belief. It is dangerous to leave this knowledge out of the many passages that connect belief and salvation. Belief and salvation are bookends of our response to grace—the sacred journey where the saving knowledge of Jesus Christ is acquired.

When Jesus says to those evildoers, "I never knew you," it indicates that they were never on the narrow road nor did they pass through the small gate. Yet they thought the whole time that they were saved, and at that moment, they fully expected to be welcomed into the kingdom. As tragic as this is, no one in our culture seems to be much worried about how the invitation is done as long as it gets results even though it creates in people a sense of entitlement. Judgment becomes a nonissue when the sacred moment of conversion (belief) is combined with the sacred moment of salvation (reward) as one event.

This has to be the essence of this passage, and I am also beginning to see this as the essence of what I was led to write in The Road to Restoration. Marketing a utopian myth politically is very similar to marketing instant salvation in that they both promise something that is not achievable in this life.

THE ABSURDITY OF GRACE

There are at least three places that Jesus uses the absurd as a teaching tool:

First, in the encounter with the Rich Ruler, he tells the man to sell all he has and give it to the poor. In the Jewish culture, this man's wealth represented his right standing with God and therefore was impossible for him to give away. In his mind, Jesus was asking him to give away his salvation.

Second, in the parable of the unmerciful servant, Jesus uses the sum of 10,000 talents, which is an amount that approaches the national debt our government has borrowed over two and a half centuries. That was such an absurd amount at that time that no one could have even imagined it.

Third, in Luke 9, Jesus tells His disciples that they must deny themselves and pick up their cross daily and follow Him. However, they all knew that you only picked up your cross one time. The next day, you were dead.

I think Jesus was using these examples to illustrate the absurdity of what He is going to do and our response. He comes to earth, teaches, and then dies on a cross to set us free from the condition of our birth. Jesus dies in the hope that we will see the magnitude of our sin debt and respond in a way that demonstrates our understanding of what He has done for us. He also teaches that we are to become disciples and kingdom builders, which is His ultimate goal. Making converts is job one, but we are also commanded to make disciples teaching obedience.

The absurdity in the parable of the unmerciful servant is that, when he receives the gift of debt forgiveness, he continues living his life as if nothing has happened or changed and may have even become more arrogant as a result of his gift (grace). This illustrates the absurdity of the response to grace in that we need only to receive it as a gift when God's grace demands much more. Instead of self-indulgence and self-service, Jesus demands self-denial and self-sacrifice in the servanthood of making Him Lord of our lives. The focus on our sin and salvation has eclipsed our response to grace and the role of God's perfect love and forgiveness is to play in our daily lives.

The demand for self-denial and self-sacrifice that Jesus puts on His disciples in Luke 9 is not in response to His death on the cross. He fails to mention His cross to His disciples when He makes this demand. It is simply a result of choosing to follow Him with the promise that choosing a life lived in service devoted to Him will result in eternal life.

The unmerciful servant, in choosing to continue to live his life as he pleased, is an example of ungrace and is the norm in today's Christian culture. It got him justice after receiving the gift of grace. Therefore, choosing to believe only brings us to the choice of how we follow, and the foundation of our faith determines that. We will likewise be held accountable.

There is no condemnation this side of the grave for those who believe, but there is condemnation at the judgment for some believers. There is a denial in the Christian culture that anyone who believes will hear these words, "I never knew you." However, I would ask you to entertain the idea that nonbelievers have condemned this side of the grave because of their unbelief and are therefore only spectators at the judgment as there is no other need for them to be there. Only believers will be judged at the judgement (John 3: 17 – 18).

Therefore, it is not unusual to be indifferent toward those who are condemned for either their nonbelief or their wrong belief. Indifference is the opposite of love, and it is evidence of the ungrace (ingratitude) of the unmerciful servant. Indifference to the lost, both inside and outside of the church, is a result of "belief, be baptized, be saved, and behave (any way you want)." The tears and anger of those "weeping and gnashing of teeth," found in Matthew 24 and 25, are not from unbelievers who have no hope.

THE SEED OF ABRAHAM

When I put all of this together, it comes out that the foundation of my salvation is in the foundation of my faith. If we would use Jesus's death on the cross for what it is, rather than massaging it and adding to it, we might find that living a life in anticipation of salvation (living in the promise made to Abraham) is much better than the idea that His work on the cross and our conversion completes His mission.

This idea is backed up by this statement found in Hebrews: "These were all commended for their faith, yet none of them received what had been promised. God had planned something better for us, so that only together with us would they be made perfect" (Hebrews 11:39–40). The promise made to Abraham is still in effect, and it's not a random event in anyone's life. We, together with those who have already been deemed righteous, all receive our eternal reward together when Jesus comes back in righteousness and final judgment.

When Jesus came to earth, the Jews were no longer living in that promise nor waiting on the fulfillment of that promise. The Sadducees didn't believe it, and the Pharisees believed they already possessed what was promised—eternal life. But both beliefs were wrong. This is the darkness that Jesus came to penetrate, the saved mindset of the Pharisees, and the unbelief of the Sadducees.

The only way to make sense of this is to say that Jesus is the light of the world, and He brings people into that light when they believe in Him as the one promised to Abraham and live in that hope until He comes back to fulfill this promise. I think that Peter captures the essence of this in 2 Peter 1:4, "Through these, He has given us His very great and precious promises, so that through them you may participate in the divine nature and escape the corruption of the world caused by evil desires."

In his faith journey, Paul had discovered, or rediscovered, the importance of living in that promise. In Galatians 3, he gives us some history, his understanding of the promise, and ends by showing us how important his understanding was: "If you belong to Christ, then you are Abraham's seed and heirs according to the promise" (verse 29). Paul had left the darkness of the Pharisees, believing that he possessed eternal life, and had come into the light of living in the promise. He is calling all of those who belong to Jesus to do the same. Living in the light of the promise made to Abraham (Messiah) and the light of being led by the Holy Spirit is the foundation of Paul's new journey. It's like walking down a dark tunnel with the light of the promise at the end and with the light of the Holy Spirit lighting the way. Living in these two lights keeps us safe as we "who through faith are shielded by God's power until the coming of the salvation that is ready to be revealed in the last time." (1 Peter 1:5).

Paul, being struck blind on the road to Damascus and then receiving his sight again, is being born again to a new vision (ref. John 3:3). He went from the darkness of being threatened by Jesus and wanting to get rid of the "Jesus sect" to the light of living in the faith and promise of the Messiah—from trying to shut up the children of the promise to become a child of the promise himself. Paul's conversion is the best example of the contrast between believing that you possess salvation and being possessed by the promise of salvation. This is the conversion that today's Christian culture desperately needs to have. Faith in the promise more than in the person—the faith of Abraham.

I have a sense that what Jesus failed to accomplish with the Pharisees as a group, He did accomplish with Paul individually. It looks to me like Paul's conversion may be a preview to the Second Coming, once again, trying to get believers back to living in the promise, rather than the possession, of eternal life.

Paul and Peter both verify that they were living in anticipation of their salvation. Paul in Romans 8:24–25 says, "For in this hope we are saved. But hope that is seen is no hope at all. Who hopes for what he already has? But if we hope for what we do not yet have, we wait for it patiently." Remember, Paul was a Pharisee who thought he was eternally secure before his encounter with Jesus.

Peter, in a much more practical way, says much the same thing: "He has given us new birth into a living hope through the resurrection of Jesus Christ from the dead, and into an inheritance that can never perish, spoil or fade—kept in heaven for you, who through faith are shielded by God's power until the coming of the salvation that is to be revealed in the last time" (1 Peter 1:3–5).

Peter very definitely puts faith and living in hope between the new birth and the salvation that is in his future. Simply stated, they lived in grace and thanksgiving for the forgiveness Jesus's death on the cross provides and in the hope and promise of their bodily resurrection upon His return. The personal nature of the conversion moment is in the person and promise of Jesus. The journey from conversion to judgment is in the person and promise of the Holy Spirit (ref. John 16:8). Hold that thought. I am about to shift gears, but promise to bring this all together in the conclusion.

CULTIVATING A KINGDOM MIND

Paul says in 1 Corinthians 2:16, "But we have the mind of Christ." I feel like God, through His Holy Spirit, has been trying to create that in me throughout my entire life, especially during these last four years while writing this book. When Jesus challenges those around Him in Luke 9:23–24 to decide to follow Him, He was an itinerant teacher claiming to be the Christ of God with no actual proof. When He talks about self-denial, picking up your cross daily not to save your life but with the promise that in losing your life you will save it, He is asking them to do something that is, at that moment, totally irrational. There was no allusion to the sacrificial nature that Jesus brings to the cross later. The only allusion is that the decision to follow Jesus will result in waking up each morning with the possibility that your day might not end well. That decision is a crisis of belief and the beginning of the new mind of becoming the new creature and losing your carnal mind literally.

Later, when Peter says to Jesus, "We have left all we had to follow you," Jesus replies, "No one who has left home, or wife, or brothers, or parents, or children for the sake of the kingdom of God will fail to receive many times as much in this age and, in the age to come, eternal life" (Luke 18:29–30). It now makes perfect sense to me that making the irrational decision to follow Jesus has the immediate effect of our moving from a carnal mind to a kingdom-mind. This decision to follow Jesus in this way will seem to be irrational to all those with carnal minds around you.

When Jesus is sweating drops that looked like blood the night of His betrayal, we get a good look inside His mind when he says, "My Father, if it is possible, may this cup be taken from me. Yet not as I will, but as you will." His mission on this earth is nearing completion, and He is facing the really hard part, but from the beginning of time, this was His destiny. Yet He wrestles with this reality, I think, for our benefit. In His humanity, Jesus is having a crisis of belief, and the sweat, like drops of blood, representing living, working and dying for the kingdom. Jesus's humanity is getting in the way of His destiny. Later, He tells Pilate that He has the power to stop the whole thing but chooses not to. This is important to me because, after He is beaten and on the way to the cross, His blood and sweat are mixed.

Jesus seems to be acting out the decision that He asks His followers to make in Luke 9:23–24. The decision to follow is to live, work, and die for the kingdom, and the faith journey that follows has those same qualities. It is a decision to stop living for yourself and to start living for the kingdom. However, it is presented today as a way to escape hell and gain heaven with belief in Jesus, all at that very moment. This becomes a sacred moment for most, if not all, Christians. But what if that moment is sacred only because the new believer is passing through the small gate that puts him on the narrow road that leads to eternal life, another sacred moment? The journey from the sacred moment of belief to the sacred moment of receiving our eternal reward then also becomes sacred.

The sacredness of the journey (narrow road) is missed because there is nothing left to do but wait. The apathy and indifference (the opposite of love) found in today's culture is a direct result of losing the sacred nature of the journey between conversion and resurrection. The gratitude for the gift of grace has been replaced by an attitude of entitlement to salvation. Paul makes this point in Romans 13:11, "And do this [love], understanding the present time. The hour has come for you to wake up from your slumber because our salvation is nearer now than when we first believed."

I have recently experienced some adversity in my own life that has helped give me this new understanding of what it means to be a follower of Jesus and to recognize that I continue to develop a new mind-set. Peter writes in the first chapter of his second letter about the things to add to your faith to develop this kingdom's mind (verses 3–11). He makes the same connection that I have that the kingdom mind (wholesome thinking) is what propels us into the kingdom. I quote these verses in "Three Days of Grace" later.

The decision to follow Jesus seems to be a choice between the consuming fire of the perishing at the judgment and the consuming presence of the fire of the Holy Spirit and dying for the kingdom right now. Working on having a kingdom mind has changed my perspective on just about everything, and I have become obsessed with being led by the Spirit in everything that I do. I love being this way, but my friends and family think that I have lost it. While some like this concept, few want to operate in this world with a kingdom-mind. They want to follow Jesus with their carnal mind, which makes so much sense and is so rational to them, but they are missing the "many times as much in this age" that comes from cultivating a kingdom-mind.

I am amazed at how closely the events of Easter follow what I perceive to be the events in a Christ follower's life—starting with the crisis of belief, then the trial, then the punishment, and picking up His cross on the way to His death, dying a human death, going into the grave, and then finally resurrection to an eternal existence. I don't believe I could see this with my carnal mind because so much of what I've heard try to focus me on myself and what Jesus did for me rather than what I am to do for Him. Heaven and hell are not the issues for the kingdom mind; living, working, and dying for the kingdom is the issue. The only issue.

In John 6:23, Jesus says, "The work of God is this: to believe in the one He has sent." Then Jesus makes it hard for them to believe, so hard in fact that all but the twelve disciples desert Him. When the believing got hard, only those twelve stuck with Him. Then Peter says, "Lord, to whom shall we go? You have the words of eternal life. We believe and know that you are the holy one of God." Later, Peter writes this: "In this, you greatly rejoice, though now for a little while, you may have had to suffer grief in all kinds of trials. These have come so that your faith…may be proved genuine and may result in praise, honor, and glory when Jesus Christ is revealed" (1 Peter 1:6–7).

Generic belief and generic faith have been substituted, and instituted, in place of the real thing. When everyone has the generic, no one seems to care about the real thing—genuine faith. I have come to the belief that there is one person more than any other that is responsible for the "believe and be saved" mindset of today.

Around the end of World War II, John Stott, a prominent English evangelist, had a great influence on evangelism by taking Revelations 3:20 out of context and using that to influence new believers with a misconception. It is the Holy Spirit knocking on the door of the lukewarm church wanting to get in, not Jesus knocking on the door of our heart, wanting to get into our heart. "Behold, I stand at the door and knock." Jesus asks the question in Luke 9, "If you would come after me" (devotedly), and He says in Matthew 7, "Knock and the door will be opened to you," a different dynamic. This misconception then plays out: how can Jesus not welcome me into the kingdom if I have invited Him into my heart? This is the grace of the lukewarm church!

The reciprocal nature of God's saving grace is being lost in a culture of entitlement to salvation, based on belief. When Jesus tells us to knock and the door will be opened to you, maybe we should see this as knocking on the door of Jesus's heart. Using this dynamic creates in me a sense of Jesus welcoming me into His heart now and into His kingdom later.

Indulge me while I unpack this absurd pretext based on regeneration at the moment of belief, instilling the saved mindset into new believers. I'm unable to open the door to Jesus without first being quickened by the Spirit. So when I am quickened by the Spirit and regenerated, at that moment, I'm saved even before I open the door. Let's just go back and read what's there, the Spirit knocking on the door of the lukewarm church—the one that He is going to spit out of His mouth and the one that is being created by this misconception. When you open the door of your heart to a lie, guess who comes in with it?

John 3:16 is then brought alongside this lie. Together, they are being used to create the "believe and be saved" culture, and the gift of eternal life becomes a participation award or trophy. The most important statement ever spoken by a human being in the history of the world is reduced to a cheap salvation statement, which it is not. Jesus is declaring, I am the one sent by God, the Messiah, the one promised to Abraham who has the power to resurrect the dead to eternal life. I like how Isaiah says it, "He will swallow up death" (Isaiah 25:8).

I have been desperate to finish this for about the past three months. Every time I think that I'm done, God seems to challenge me to sharpen up some point. I have begun to think of this as sharpening the hoe to cut off the head of the snake, but He never seemed to give me what I considered to be that fatal blow. After writing that last paragraph, I went home and then to a Wednesday night Bible study in a Baptist church that I attend. As I listened to John in 1 John 3:14, there it was.

Listen to what John says about regeneration: "We know that we have passed from death to life because we love our brothers. Anyone who does not love remains in death." It seems to me that John gives us the task of making secure the promise of salvation by loving our brothers. Those who don't get this, put themselves in the "I never knew you" crowd.

I am saved by grace, but only by extension. The grace that saves me is the grace that I extend to all those around me. Read around this, and you'll find John's definition of grace and the importance of sinless obedience, commanding us to believe, to love, and to forgive others as Christ loved and forgave us. This is the legal tender, the currency of the kingdom, and a matter of obedience: forgiving the unforgivable, loving the unlovable.

In Matthew 10:7–8, Jesus captures the essence of the gospel of grace when He says this: "As you go, preach this message, 'The kingdom of heaven is near.' Heal the sick, raise the dead, cleanse those who have leprosy, drive out demons. Freely have you received, freely give."

LIVING GRACEFULLY
IN THE AGE OF GRACE

When Jesus says while on the cross, "It is finished," it is easy for me to believe that He is referring to the end of Daniel's sixty-ninth week. God hits the Pause button in His plan of restoration, and humanity enters into the untimed age of grace (a.k.a. the Church Age). God will take His finger off the Pause button at Jesus's return in the final judgment. Daniel's seventieth week (the Tribulation) ends the age of grace. At this time, God's righteousness and judgment prevail.

From the time of our conversion to our natural death, we have the opportunity to live a life worthy of our calling and this gift of grace. Many passages speak to this, but most, if not all people are trying to find ways to respond to their salvation. We need to focus on being worthy of the gift of grace that makes salvation, justified by grace, possible. When we do that, we will become the grace-filled people of the kingdom right now.

I experience grace as two distinct gifts, connected but received at different moments. At Jesus's death, I received God's perfect love and forgiveness, grace freely given. At Jesus's return, I will receive God's perfect love in the resurrection, ultimate grace, but not freely given. It's like I'm born with a truckload of sugar cubes (the grace of the cross). I am to give those sugar cubes away (God's perfect love) every time I get the chance before my death and promised resurrection.

The sacredness of the journey between conversion and salvation is being missed by making them one event. Peter says, "Your faith… of greater worth than gold…may be proved genuine and may result in praise, glory, and honor when Jesus is revealed." This speaks to the reward that Jesus promises to Peter in this age and also indicates the sacredness of those things between his new birth and Jesus' Second Coming.

The three tellings of the Rich Ruler all mention this reward. The carnal mind cannot grasp this idea of being rewarded for making living, working, and dying for the kingdom more important than the things we treasure most in this world. Only a kingdom mind can grasp this demand; only a kingdom mind, empowered by the Holy Spirit, can make this happen, and only a kingdom mind can say to Jesus, "We have left everything to follow you!"

When the moment of conversion and salvation are combined into one event, the age of grace becomes the age of "I'm saved and you're not." How very ungrateful. The age of salvation does not happen until Jesus comes back and says face-to-face who is saved and who is not. This ends the age of grace and begins the age to come. My divine appointment is in my future. It's when I hope to hear Jesus say to me face-to-face, "Come [Thomas], you who are blessed by my Father; take your inheritance, the kingdom prepared for you since the creation of the world" (Matthew 25:24). I'm not going to allow anyone playing God to tell me what Jesus wants to tell me Himself, "but, he who stands firm to the end will be saved" (Matthew 24:13).

THREE DAYS OF GRACE

I have come to view grace in a way that seems rather unique and may help explain the point of all of this. It is a parental pattern of God's grace with the promise of reward being the key factor. The first day of grace is what God did through Jesus on the cross—Friday. The grace of the cross and the promise of salvation with instructions on how to live, love and forgive. The second day of grace is man's response to the first day of grace—Saturday or Sabbath. This includes man's obedience or disobedience (spiritual warfare) to God in daily living, the Spirit-led journey of our natural life. The third day of grace is the grace of accountability, the fulfillment of the divine promise, and resurrection—Sunday. Three days of grace, each one wholly dependent on the other, equally important and equally sacred.

In his second letter, Peter captures perfectly these three days of grace. Look especially at how he begins and ends his description of his second day of grace. "His divine power has given us everything we need for life and godliness through our knowledge of him who called us by his glory and goodness. Through these, he has given us his very great and precious promises, so that through them you may participate in the divine nature and escape the corruption in the world caused by evil desires. For this very reason, make every effort to add to your faith; goodness…knowledge…self-control…

perseverance…godliness…brotherly kindness…love [agape]. For if you possess these qualities in increasing measure, they will keep you from being ineffective and unproductive… Therefore, my brothers, be all the more eager to make your election sure. For if you do these things, you will never fall, and you will receive a rich welcome into the eternal kingdom of our Lord and Savior Jesus Christ" (2 Peter 1:3–11).

There is so much joy in Peter's words here, telling us to "make your calling and election sure" and to enjoy living in anticipation, expectation, and confidence of a rich welcome into the kingdom. Peter's instructions seem to direct us into the center of God's will and thus into the center of His kingdom later. Jesus places Peter in the center of God's will at the very last, not by using guilt over past failures, but by "Do you love me… Feed my sheep." Jesus reinstates Peter with love, not guilt.

Let's take a moment and look at Jesus teaching us about ungrace. Hidden in the parable of the prodigal (Luke 15) is a picture of ungrace. We don't want to notice the older brother because his reaction would not stand out in today's culture. He demonstrates an inability to forgive and to love his brother because of what his younger brother had done. The story ends with the father and older brother standing outside of the party arguing in the dark.

It is only in the power of the Holy Spirit that the older brother can find the grace to overcome the resentment that he feels. He needs to love and forgive his brother as perfectly as the father does, and it is only then that he can go back into the party and celebrate. The younger brother was lost—he knew it and came home. The older brother stayed home, was lost, and didn't know it. I have said this before, and I'll say it again, Jesus says that if we don't forgive, we will not be forgiven, and John says that if we don't love (our brother), we remain in death (darkness).

The stark contrast of the father's love and the son's resentment is the lesson in grace here. The older son is miserable and can't get over himself and his need to see his brother punished. He has the perfect opportunity to love his brother just as the father does. He has received the father's perfect love but can't extend it to his brother. It is only in loving his brother that he can come out of the darkness and into the celebration.

Don't miss the fact that at that moment, he is angry with his father for the grace freely given to his brother. He wants justice for his brother and resents his father for not doing just that. The younger brother could not live in the grace of the promise of the inheritance. The older brother could not live in the grace of the father's love and forgiveness, freely given to his brother.

What I see in the older brother is what I see in the saved mindset of the Pharisees and the same saved mindset I see in the culture around me. Instead of a growing love for the father and his lost brother, we find a growing resentment and the "what about me" attitude of "where is my fatted calf?" This brings to light a benign entitlement that comes with the saved mindset, and maybe the most important thing—he is missing the joy of giving and receiving the father's perfect love and forgiveness.

In his moment of clarity, the younger brother loses his sense of entitlement and gains a servant's heart when he says to himself, "Father… I am no longer worthy to be called your son; make me one of your hired men." He never gets the chance to say what he is rehearsing before his father runs to him, and showers him, with love, affection, and forgiveness… When our focus is in making converts and bringing people into the church, entitlement is a good selling point. But if our focus is on making disciples and bringing people into the kingdom, entitlement is the worst place to start.

I think Luther tried to explain grace to the Catholic Church as Wesley tried to explain grace to the Calvinists. Can it be that our human nature tries to find another path to the kingdom to avoid living in the grace that saves us? Also, can it be that when we are convinced that we are entitled to salvation by works or belief or deciding to accept Jesus or joining the Christian culture, etc., we become learning disabled in our understanding of what it means to become, like Paul, a child of the promise of salvation?

As a leader, John Wesley did a lot of work toward helping people understand grace. As a mentor, he put "holy clubs" (classes) in place so that people could educate themselves as to what was in the Bible. It was truly a grassroots movement with people working out their salvation and not being told what to believe. It may be that the church is being pushed back into a similar situation, and house churches' holy clubs will once again come against the Christian culture as it now exists. Let's put a new face on the Christian culture and start believing that it is grace, through faith, that saves us.

I don't think we can find the desired relationship with God in scripture unless it is in learning to live in His grace by extending His perfect love and forgiveness to others. This shared sacrifice may be where the relationship is reborn and where we will find the joy of serving Him. Living in grace may be the only way for us to live out our lives and share in His suffering, both at the same time. Grace starts as shared suffering on the way to shared joy. One of the points that Peter makes in his second letter is to associate the qualities of graceful living, or lack thereof, to shortsightedness and forgetting the grace of having our sins forgiven (ref. 2 Peter 1:9).

A good example of the choice between living in thanksgiving for the grace we are given and taking it for granted is in the life of Pat Tillman in an act of patriotism. He was an undersized star linebacker for the Arizona Cardinals. He had it all: he lived his life passionately, had a beautiful family, had a million-dollar contract, and lived the American dream. The events of 9/11 so affected him that he set all of those aside to join the Army Rangers and go to war—a decision that ultimately cost him his life when he was killed by friendly fire. A documentary was done on his life. It depicts him as one having a childlike exuberance and enthusiasm that he brought to everything he did. I see in his story all the elements of living passionately for the eternal kingdom that Jesus describes in our deciding to follow him.

PROGRESSIVE CHRISTIAN EVANGELISTIC MYTHOLOGY

The end game in marketing is closing the deal. The "decision theology" that has grown up around this technique has deciding to believe in Jesus and thereby receiving salvation the primary focus of evangelists, and of the Christian Culture. The critical issue in salvation is your decision to follow Jesus. While this is secondary to belief, it is primary in receiving the promise of salvation. The decision to follow Jesus is not something that fits well into this modern marketing plan because the cost of discipleship is a deal-breaker and must be minimized or ignored to close the deal. God's plan of restoring us to paradise hinges on how we follow, not on what we believe. Because of this, our culture is just as misguided today about His Second Coming as the Jewish culture that Jesus came into was at His First Coming.

The Jewish Culture (Pharisees) had used the blood of the sacrificial lamb and the law, combined with the blood of Abraham running in their veins, to make themselves right with God and to achieve eternal security. The blood of the lamb did not achieve both as they also needed the righteousness of Abraham's blood. It was a Jewish myth that the blood of Abraham, a Gentile, made them righteous as it was not Abraham's blood that made him righteous but his faith in a promise made to him by God. The Jews seemed to have forgotten that fact. At the judgment, we need Jesus's righteousness to be clothed in His righteousness, faultless before the throne, just like Abraham. The Pharisees could not get their heads out of the sand of believing that they were already saved.

It follows that the goal is not in achieving salvation on this side of the grave. He gives us a lifetime to show our gratitude for His sacrifice in paying our sin debt. The sacred moments along this journey are the moments of self-denial, self-sacrifice, living, working, and dying for the kingdom. Telling people that at the start of their journey (modern Calvinism), they have escaped hell and gained heaven robs them of all of the sacred moments of that journey. This is the head of the snake that needs to be chopped off because the Jewish myth has been reborn in our culture. A myth is a lie that takes on a life of its own. In the area of religion, I see this as misguided "group thinking." We cannot escape the coming wrath by any other means than to live gracefully in the age of grace and the light of God's promise to Abraham.

In 1 Corinthians 15, Paul deals with the importance of Christ's resurrection to one's faith and hope. In this chapter, he says something that I believe has been missed by the Christian culture: "I declare to you, brothers, that flesh and blood cannot inherit the kingdom of God, nor does the perishable inherit the imperishable" (verse 50). As I read this and all that Paul writes here, it occurs to me that if Jesus dies and does not come out of the grave, the promise of eternal life would die with Him. In Christ's death, burial, and resurrection, the promise made to Abraham—eternal life—is also brought back to life. Easter is not the fulfillment of the promise—it is the resurrection of the promise.

So often when I talk to friends about dying and going into the grave, they bring up the thief on the cross. "I tell you the truth, today you will be with me in paradise." If you place the comma after today, you change the meaning of what Jesus is saying. When you look at what the thief says—"Jesus, remember me when you come into your kingdom"—the focus shifts to Jesus's Second Coming. Jesus's response then becomes He doesn't need to remember; He can make him the promise right now and at that time he, the thief, will come out of the dust and be welcomed into paradise.

I believe this is kingdom thinking. Delayed gratification is not gratification denied. It is the gratification that doesn't appeal to the carnal mind. Where you individually place the comma identifies where your mind is and where you are on your journey. Can it be just that simple? When you move that comma, it has the effect of moving the carnal mind to a kingdom mind, and for me, it reflects how my focus has changed and what my faith is truly all about.

When I started writing, I was unaware of the controversy about where to put the comma. It's an old one, but it may be pivotal in identifying who you are in Christ. One side is the instant gratification received at the moment that you believe you get the keys to the kingdom, and at the moment you die, you go to heaven. The other side, at the moment that you believe you begin growing in grace, knowledge, and the promise of salvation, and at the moment you die, you go into the grave having put your trust in Jesus to judge and reward you at His Second Coming. "Rock my soul in the bosom of Abraham."

The instant-gratification crowd has missed the point of that encounter entirely. As they hang there in all that pain, Jesus tells him that this is not all there is. No matter how good or bad your life is, there is a paradise that awaits those who put their trust in Him. This is the same promise God made to Abraham 2000 years earlier. It is a hope and a promise worth waiting for, and it is a hope and promise worth sharing. From the beginning of time, God had planned to show that it was a hope and a promise worth dying for.

In this chapter, I believe I have captured how differently Scripture is interpreted by those whose faith is focused on sin and salvation and those who's faith begins a sacred journey focused on lordship.

EMBRACING THE SAVED
MIND-SET OF THE PHARISEES

It is very clear to me that today's misguided evangelists, in lockstep (Revelation 3:20 and John 3:16), have continued to bring the Christian culture to the same place that the Jews were when Jesus said to them, "You diligently study the Scriptures because you think by them you possess eternal life. These are the scriptures that testify about me, yet you refuse to come to me and have life" (John 5:39–40).

The mind-set that Jesus is dealing with here is that the Jews were God's chosen people, His elect to the exclusion of all others, and the Pharisees believed they had eternal security. This idea reemerged with John Calvin. Man is helpless to believe and must be chosen by God to believe, become His elect, and at the moment of belief, be saved and eternally secure. The Pharisees making salvation a possession and an entitlement was a step too far. It is at this point that the Pharisees become children of the devil, not looking for the one promised to Abraham to bring resurrection but one to save them from the curse, the rule of the Romans. If you have been taught that belief is the evidence of salvation and at your death, you are entitled to the kingdom, your faith is a mirror image of the faith of the Pharisees.

A life lived in an unfulfilled promise of resurrection made to Abraham had died in the Jewish culture. They either didn't believe it, or they believed they were entitled to it. Either way, it was effectively no longer a promise to be lived in; it was something to be possessed or ignored. Using Satan's tools, truth sprinkled with lies. The Jews had stopped living in the light of the promise of the Messiah. Jesus had to come out of heaven, knock one of them off his mule, strike him blind to get his attention, get him back to the promise, and to impress that into his brain. Once one has the saved mindset, you would have to move heaven and earth to change it. I think Paul is spinning in his grave to think that our teachers have cherry-picked the New Testament scriptures to the same end.

Trying not to put God in a box and maybe thinking way outside the box, several things occur to me. Does Jesus need to come at all if the Jews were still living in the promise of, and waiting on, the one promised to Abraham to bring eternal life? Why is it okay for Christians to believe that they can possess salvation when it wasn't okay for the Jews, especially in light of what the writer of Hebrews says about His Second Coming, "to bring salvation to those who are waiting on him"? I've often wondered why Jesus had to die this horrible death. It is now beginning to make sense to me that His death also represents the death of living a life in the promise of salvation. Would it have been easier for the Jews to recognize Him, believe in Him, and not be threatened by Him if they had not had their saved mind-set?

It is instructive to connect the saved mindset of the Pharisees to a warning about evangelism: "Woe to you teachers of the law and Pharisees, you hypocrites! You shut the kingdom of heaven in men's faces. You yourselves do not enter, nor will you let those enter who are trying to… You travel over land and sea to win a single convert, and when he becomes one, you make him twice as much as a son of hell as you are" (Matthew 23:13–16). It is not a stretch to believe that Jesus has a problem with the marketing of salvation (ref. John 2:16). There is no evidence that the Jews had ever done the evangelism that Jesus is describing here. There is the possibility that Jesus is guarding against future evangelists creating in others the saved mindset of the Pharisees and locking themselves and their converts out of the kingdom. There is no other reason that I can think of for Jesus to say something that is not true at that time. However, this surely has come true in our time.

This is in contrast to Jesus's instructions for today's evangelists to teach obedience: "Therefore, go and make disciples of all nations… teaching them to obey all that I have commanded you" (Matthew 28:19–20). Obedience is the evidence of faith and, therefore, the foundation of lordship and salvation. I think it is also instructive to look to see if your faith lines up with Paul's faith before his conversion or after. It is a black-and-white issue. You are either a child of the promise, or you are not.

I think it is worth noting here that whether you agree with how I have put this together or not, Jesus is pointing out that after conversion, one can become a double son of hell, depending on what is taught, moving from the darkness of unbelief to the darkness of wrong belief. Peter makes this same point differently but comes to the same conclusion (ref. 2 Peter 2:20–22). Read what Peter says about this starting in verse 17 and let Peter add context to what Jesus said.

These two passages come closest to describing the depraved condition that I hear about so much. It's not that we start that way in our spiritual journey but that we can be misled and, like the Pharisees, end up that way—the children of Abraham becoming the sons of hell. It is a world of make-believe, pretending you already have something that is yet to come. When Paul writes about the inability of mankind to come out of the darkness of unbelief, he most likely is writing about the darkness that he came out of—the darkness of wrong belief that had taken over the Jewish culture.

Since I am a skeptic by nature and believe that Wesley was right in believing that Calvin was wrong, I see Jesus warning us about moving from the unbelieving mindset of the Sadducees to the believing saved mindset of the Pharisees. This is something that happens in an instant for those who follow Calvin: instantly going from the darkness of unbelief to the darkness of wrong belief of being eternally secure, having the saved mindset of the Pharisees.

The passage that has most influenced my thinking on becoming "a child of the promise" is Hebrews 9:27–28: "Just as man is destined to die once, and after that to face judgment, so Christ was sacrificed once to take away the sins of many people, and He will appear a second time, not to bear sin, but to bring salvation to those who are waiting on Him." It seems to me that the Jews' inability to live in the light of the promise of eternal life (Messiah) results in God, through Jesus, extending that invitation and promise to the whole world. Now, it's the whole world that needs to live in the light of the promise.

The Holy Spirit could not work in the hearts of the Pharisees who believed they possessed eternal life. He can only work in the hearts of the truly lost or those who live in the light of the promise of eternal life and, like Paul, become "children of the promise." It may be helpful to read what Paul says about being children of the promise and Abraham's offspring in Romans 9:6–9. Here, Paul connects being a child of the promise and a child of Abraham to the promise that Sarah would have a son.

Out of Sarah's impatience with God fulfilling that promise, we get Ishmael—evidence of how difficult it was for Sarah to live in a promise made to her by God. The hostility in the Middle

East today is a direct result of Sarah's impatience with God and His promise. It is easy for me to connect this episode to Eve being seduced in the Garden and she and Adam losing access to the Tree of Life, thus losing what that represents and would become the promise of eternal life. God chooses to make that promise a reality for Abraham and Sarah, Isaac and Jacob, and to the nation of Israel.

Jesus says in Matthew 8:10–12, "I tell you the truth, I have not found anyone in Israel with such great faith. I say to you that many will come from the east and the west, and will take their places at the feast with Abraham, Isaac, and Jacob in the kingdom of heaven, but the subjects of the kingdom [Jewish heirs] will be thrown outside, into darkness, where there will be weeping and gnashing of teeth." I believe that Jesus is addressing the consequences for the Jews drifting away from the faith of Abraham and living in the light of the promise of salvation. The weeping and gnashing of teeth is the result of Jews who stopped living in the promise of salvation. There is a parallel between what Jesus is saying here about the Jews and what He says about those who fail to do likewise at His Second Coming in Matthew 24 and 25.

Those who are in the business of saving souls have used John Calvin as their mentor and maybe a flawed view of Paul's conversion as their guide. They have created in too many people the saved mindset of the Pharisees and lost the elements of hope and promise that runs so deeply throughout both the Old and New Testaments. God used the events of Easter and Paul's subsequent conversion to make the kingdom available to the whole world. The promise did not change nor was it fulfilled. It was just extended to the whole world.

BIRTHING THE KINGDOM ON EARTH RIGHT NOW

The Jews were under the rule of the Romans, and this represents the curse God put on His creation. Their prayer was that God would send them a savior to save them from the Romans. Their focus on the curse of the Romans was the main cause of them not getting Jesus and thus missing the promise of eternal life in the age to come. In a sense, the Jews' fear of the Roman cross and their saved mindset were the main elements that put Jesus on the cross.

"Do not be afraid of those who can kill the body but cannot kill the soul. Rather, be afraid of the One who can destroy both soul and body in hell" (Matthew 19:28). We don't like to look at God in this way, and I think today this would be better understood by saying, "Don't be afraid of those things that can kill the body." Here, Jesus may be talking about Himself since He is the one who comes in righteousness and judgment.

Allowing the fear of death and the things of the curse to rule over our lives puts us in bondage to Satan. Dying to that fear brings the freedom to serve the one who has the power over life and death. Choosing to live in the promise of salvation helps me find ways to die to my fear of death and focus on my relationship with the One. This, in turn, secures my place in the kingdom. I need to be motivated by the desire to build the relationship and the fear of losing the relationship.

Most of the prayers that I hear in church deal with the things of the curse. The fear of pain, death, sickness, imprisonment (both physical and emotional) all seem to rule our lives. I see a parallel here with the Jews and believe that Jesus's promise of the kingdom and release from the curse in the age to come is also a promise for the present. We will be surrounded by the kingdom in the age to come, but what about right now? I believe that those who are destined for the kingdom do not fear the things of the curse and have a promise of that same existence right now.

In Luke 12:32, we find that promise. Surrounded by instruction for the present we find this: "Do not be afraid, little flock, for your Father has been pleased to give you the kingdom." When you make Jesus Lord of your life, that kingdom comes and dwells inside, and the promise that the kingdom of God is within you comes true. Imagining how it will be in the kingdom free from the curse is a waste unless you use that image to rule over your life right now.

All that I have written points to this very simple truth. That if you make Jesus Christ Lord of your life and that is your single focus, you do not have to worry about salvation. Salvation takes care of itself. That mindset is incompatible with Calvinism since lordship is impossible without first being saved. I touched on this in The Road to Restoration but did not realize at that time how pivotal this is. The reality of this simple truth, or theology, is one cannot market salvation since it is 100 percent God's business, and no one knows who the saved are until Jesus comes back and reveals just who is saved and who is not. They both can't be true as one must be a heresy.

You will find evidence of this in your own life when you see a believer doing wrong and wondering or worrying about their salvation. You are seeing the fatal flaw of being a born-again believer that continues to be lord of their own life. The reason this is fatal is that we seldom, if ever, see this in ourselves.

God used the saved mindset of the teachers of the law and the Pharisees as a reason to bring about a radical shift in how the relationship between God and mankind would be restored. Sending Jesus to correct the saved mind-set of those leaders was part of God's plan to extend the promise to the Gentiles and thus to you and me. I embrace this correction, but instead of living in the promise of salvation and embracing that, the Christian culture seems more and more to be embracing the saved mindset of the Pharisees. Those who focus on and/or market salvation have won over the culture, telling us what we want to hear.

John Calvin created a theology that appeals to man's instant self-gratification nature using possession, entitlement, and eternal security as motivators. I have used the same tools to come to a different conclusion than he did. I know when I started writing that I disagreed with Calvin's predestination and eternal security concepts but did not know why beyond my human understanding. In the process of writing this, God has given me the reasoning and understanding to know why and the means to share this rediscovered understanding with the whole world.

History proves that I am on very firm ground. I feel like I am standing on the shoulders of John Wesley who stood on the shoulders of Jacobus Arminius who stood on the shoulders of Paul, each one coming against the saved mindset of the Pharisees in their own time and in their way. The darkness that Jesus came to penetrate is still with us, both in those who believe in the resurrection from the dead as well as those who don't.

From the time I first encountered the idea of predestination, I have thought of it as fatalism. Man's eternal destination is determined before he is born, Calvin's limited atonement. The saved mindset that grows out of this was spiritually fatal to the Pharisees who thought salvation was their birthright. It distresses me a great deal to believe that God has led me to this conclusion: that the saved mindset of today, a born-again birthright, is fatal to all who have it. A life lived in the promise of salvation was Abraham's salvation.

I have no idea when I decided to believe this way, but I do know this book would not have been written if I had bought into the instant-gratification, carnal mindset that I found to be contrary to what I read and now believe. I know that as I was writing, I hoped that I would be able to challenge the readers and give them a chance to self-identify as to which faith journey seemed to be right for them. I hope and pray I have done that.

The encounter with the Rich Ruler had to break Jesus's heart as he walked away even if the question was insincere: "What must I do to inherit eternal life?" Today's "believe and be saved" culture doesn't want to hear "follow me." They would rather hear, "Just sincerely believe in me, ask me into your heart, and the kingdom is yours." But no, "follow me" is the answer Jesus gave him. Following Jesus, being led by the Spirit, as a devoted child of the promise of salvation is the only answer.

> "At that time Jesus said, 'I praise you, Father, Lord of heaven and earth, because you have hidden-den these things from the wise and learned, and revealed them to little children. Yes, for this was your good pleasure'" (Matthew 11:25–26).

> "And he said: 'I tell you the truth unless you change and become like little children, you will never enter the kingdom of heaven'" (Matthew 18:3).

"Yet to all who received him, to those who believed in his name, he gave the right to become children of God—children born not of natural descent, nor of human decision or a husband's will, but born of God" (John 1:12–13).

"To him who overcomes, I will give the right to eat from the tree of life, which is in the paradise of God" (Revelation 2:7).

RUMINATING

Pushing Back

When one looks for gold or anything of value, it is always found in the last place you look. This is to say that once you find what you're looking for, you stop looking. In one's spiritual journey, when you find the place you've been looking for, a place of comfort and security, you'll stop looking any further. It is evident that the darkness that Jesus came to penetrate in the Jewish culture was their comfort spot, and they pushed back. The Roman spear that was pushed into Jesus's side represents that pushback, making sure that He was dead. This is the darkness pushing back at the light.

When we meet Paul (Saul), he is continuing the pushback. He is out to make sure that the darkness Jesus came to penetrate continues. But then, at his conversion, he starts pushing against the darkness that he just came out of. I believe the thorn in Paul's side may have been his way of cryptically acknowledging the pain of his change of direction and what he had done before his conversion.

Pushing against the darkness that had become a very comfortable place for the Jews was a monumental task. When Paul chose to push against the darkness of the Romans, they pushed back and killed him. Anytime people feel like they have found a comfortable and secure place, they will fight any attempt to move them. When I use Bible passages, especially from Hebrews, to come against the idea of salvation at the moment of conversion, I get the same push-back. It's as if no one can grasp the reality of the Pharisees and Jesus's real-life encounter with Nicodemus. That encounter in John 3 was about pushing against the darkness of his saved mind-set. If those who believe in Jesus could grasp that one thing, they would discard that mind-set quickly and start living in and being possessed by the light of the promise of salvation.

Jesus ends the Beatitudes (Matthew 5) with this: "Blessed are those who are persecuted for righteousness sake for theirs is the kingdom of heaven." This and the next two verses speak to the push-back that followers will encounter as they seek God's righteousness. I believe that the water that comes out of Jesus when the spear is pushed into his side could represent that pushback. I can't help but connect this to what Jesus says in John 3: "Unless a man is born of water and the Spirit, he cannot enter the kingdom of heaven." Paul promises that we will be persecuted (ref. 2 Timothy 3:12), and to me, this says that we will be baptized in the water of pushback. It's God seeking those who worship in Spirit and truth in John 4—it's the water welling up to eternal life. It's the "river of the water of life" that we find in Revelation 22.

I want you to know that from the very beginning of my writing "The Road To Restoration" I have been led to pushing back at the idea of eternal security and having a saved mind-set. So what am I pushing for? A theology based on Arminian Contra-Calvinism, which in denominational terms might be labeled as Advent-Wesleyan. It would be a community of faith focused on righting wrongs in our society (social justice) with this common understanding: looking forward to the Second Coming when Jesus "brings salvation to those who are waiting for Him" (Hebrews

9:28). Just before I sent this to the editing process, I came across something golden: "Salvation through Jesus, A Lifelong Process"

> Salvation begins with the work of Jesus Christ on the cross, but it expresses itself throughout- out the life of the believer. Salvation is a lifelong process that unites the believer with God to become part of the divine. This process of salvation culminates when Christ returns to judge the world and the bodies of Christians are raised from the dead and transformed, just as Christ's physical body was raised and transformed.

This thought comes from the Orthodox tradition and predated Calvinist tradition. It opposes Catholic tradition and seems to reinforce my idea of a sacred journey between two sacred moments.

Jesus said of the Jews of his time, "You belong to your father, the devil" (John 8:44). That is in contrast to Him saying that Abraham, Isaac, and Jacob would be in the kingdom. Instead of passing from death to life, over the centuries, the Jews had passed from life to death, the opposite of regeneration. Living in the light of the promise of salvation had degenerated into living in the darkness of believing they were God's elect, eternally secure. In Acts 7, Stephen captures this journey as he takes the Sanhedrin, and us, on that same journey. Their descent into darkness was systematic and deliberate as they stopped living in the light of the promise. It is very evident they thought they were already eternally secure a long time ago and killed all those who rained on their parade. Why else would they kill the prophets who reminded them of, and predicted, the coming of the promised Righteous One?

Stephen is talking to Sadducees and Pharisees alike. Both groups, and the beliefs that they held, were guilty of this descent into darkness. They had reinvented the word messiah. It was now to be someone who would come and serve them. They wanted God to send someone (a king) to fight their battles to save them from the Romans.

Living in the light of the promise and living in the light of the Holy Spirit are brought together in this passage (Acts 7) and are inseparable. A life lived in the darkness of the possession of salvation is a life lived resisting the Holy Spirit and thus the same as not having the Spirit at all. When I bring the definition of faith found in Hebrews alongside this, it becomes clear what is being said about the faith of Abraham. "Now faith is being sure of what is hoped for and certain of what we do not see" (Hebrews 11:1). Living in the light of the hope and promise of resurrection and the light of the unseen presence of God, namely the Holy Spirit, is the faith of Abraham. Once it is understood that Easter is not a complete work of salvation, it is easy to see and then model the faith of Abraham. This is Paul's conversion—going from the darkness of the possession of salvation to the light of living in the promise of salvation, the faith of Abraham.

Sometimes I think Paul, being a theologian, missed the simplicity of what God was showing him. The faith of Abraham is so simple to understand that even a child can grasp it. Believing in a kingdom far away has all the elements of a fairytale except that it is a promised reality for all those who have the faith of Abraham. It's the difference between taking the mystery element out of what is promised by making it possession and leaving the mystery element in the fairytale ending and dreaming about the kingdom that is to come.

If the apple is a metaphor for paradise, then the bite of the apple is a taste of paradise taken in disobedience. Taking the mystery out of God's promise of paradise is Satan's game plan. Receiving the promise of paradise is the beginning of a relationship with God where obedience to His plan of salvation is equally shared by His people and His Son. The world is constantly pushing against the idea that we should patiently wait for anything. Instant gratification is at war with the promise being fulfilled.

THE FOOLISH DEBATE

The debate over when salvation happens maybe Satan's way of taking our attention away from the main thing. All that is said about the promise of salvation is not there to debate when it happens; it's there to motivate people to make Jesus Lord of their lives. There is an irony in this that the promise of eternal life is what draws us to the God of Abraham, but the Promised One Jesus becomes a stumbling block to those who have not made Him Lord of their lives. For those who have made Jesus Lord of their lives, salvation is no longer the issue. The issue is making Him Lord of our lives and, moment by moment, keeping Him there.

In Romans 10:9, Paul writes, "That if you confess with your mouth, 'Jesus is lord,' and believe in your heart that God raised Him from the dead, you will be saved." Those who want to debate and focus on salvation have missed Paul's point in Romans 9 and 10 entirely. I believe that God has led me to make the same point to my generation that Paul is making to his generation in this passage. For me, this is Paul's way of saying that, if you make Jesus Lord of your life, salvation takes care of itself. He is dealing with his Jewish brother's refusal to believe and to make Jesus Lord and is using every argument that he can think of to motivate them to make that decision. I find it interesting that Paul says this right in the middle of the passage where the debate centers on how and when salvation happens.

I put the picture of a broken arrow on the cover to represent God's people not living in the promise. It is evident that God is serious about His people living in the promise of salvation and not claiming it as a done deal. When we as a culture have taken possession of what is promised, isn't that the same as the stolen bite of the apple that broke the relationship to begin with and thus the breaking of the promise?

Making Jesus Lord of your life is not a matter of belief—it is a matter of will. God gives us a lot of help to get to the place where we say, "Not my will, but your will be done." Allowing God to bend my will to His is the divine process, or journey, to the kingdom. The day of salvation is not a divine moment in time that goes into the past. Living each day in a divine promise, seeking God's will in all that is done, is a way of life. My will and God's will come together to secure my place in the kingdom.

The importance of understanding Paul's conversion cannot be overemphasized. He did not go from unbelief to belief. He went from wrong belief to right belief. That right belief was in the Promised One he met on the road to Damascus and living in the promise God made to Abraham. Jesus was not just a nice addition to what he already believed. He came out of that darkness into the light of living in the promise God made to Abraham two thousand years earlier. Two thousand years later, he and Abraham are still in the grave waiting on that promise to be fulfilled (ref. Hebrews 11:39).

Just before his conversion, Paul had been reminded of the faith of Abraham by Stephen's speech as he was about to be stoned. I think it can be assumed that Paul was listening to Stephen's speech, which was still fresh in his mind at his encounter with Jesus. It is easy for me to believe that this is where God was leading Paul in his faith journey. Paul was to model his faith after Abraham's and to believe that Jesus was the Promised One, the Messiah.

Together these two events are what God used to make the promise of resurrection available to the whole world. Paul's conversion is therefore moving from salvation through Abraham's blood to salvation through Abraham's faith. There are two issues here: what it takes to get us on the right path and what it takes to get us into the kingdom. Focusing on what it took to get into the kingdom had sent the Jews into the darkness that Jesus came to penetrate. They had left the faith of Abraham behind.

Jesus addresses this in John 8:30–47. To those who had put their faith in Him and believed in Him, He still takes issue with them. However, they continue to believe that salvation is their birthright, they have no room in their lives for His Word (the Word made flesh) and that Abraham's faith was different from theirs. It is clear that Jesus was not going to be a nice addition to what they already believed and that they needed to make Jesus Himself God and Lord of their life. Belief and faith get you started, but lordship is what gets you into the kingdom.

I think this is where being a child of the promise is so important. It puts us in a God–God's child relationship. This is what was lost in Eden, "And the Lord God said, 'The man has now become like one of us, knowing good and evil. He must not be allowed to reach out his hand and take also from the tree of life and eat, and live forever'" (Gen 3:22). Adam and Eve, at that moment, became disobedient children of the promise of eternal life without any hope. This is the human condition until we put our hope in Jesus and live in that hope until He comes back to fulfill that promise. Without being "born anew to a living hope" (Peter), we remain hopeless and disobedient.

When I read John 5:24–29, I see two moments of regeneration. First, the moment of belief passing from the hopelessness of unbelief to the hope in Jesus to fulfill the promise of eternal life. For the Jews, it was the hopelessness of wrong belief. Second, at Jesus's Second Coming, He fulfills that promise. Speaking to those in the grave, the dead are raised from death to life, regenerated to eternal life—the result of doing good (the sacred journey between two sacred moments) and living in the promise God made to Abraham. This passage defeats the idea that belief is the evidence of salvation and the moment you die you go to heaven. Jesus is echoing the prophet Daniel with more detail, which I quoted to end The Road to Restoration.

In verse 29, Jesus connects doing good and evil to our reward. This has to be about who was doing the good and evil, not about what was done since our works are unto righteousness, not salvation. Jesus says elsewhere that those He is talking to are children of the devil and thus their deeds are evil. Paul equates being a child of God with being a child of the promise and thus their deeds are good in His eyes. Jesus points out in verse 39 that those he is talking to, the Pharisees, are children of the possession of salvation, and this may be what this passage is all about—raised to a life lived in the promise of salvation (good) or to a condemned life lived in the possession of salvation (evil). This saved mindset is sacred to all those who have it. Jesus starts this passage by saying, "I tell you the truth, whoever hears my word and believes." He knows that the Jewish leaders are not listening to Him, but I'm glad John was. As far as the Jews were concerned, Jesus was wasting His breath as they plotted to kill Him. This could be a test for today's culture. If you think you get the keys to the kingdom at the moment you believe and at the moment you die, you go to heaven, the question begs to ask, are you listening?

As I look at today's Christian culture where lifestyle doesn't seem to matter, I see the holiness that John Wesley aspired to and preached disappearing. Part of Calvin's theology is that all righteousness is imputed, that we have no righteousness of our own, that even after conversion/salvation, the sinful life would or could continue. The word for this is antinomianism, which means "without the law" or "lawlessness." This made Calvin's theology very attractive in that one could continue to be lord of their own life with no change required. Becoming a law unto yourself best describes what happens to those who have a saved mindset and why the Jewish leaders had become children of their father, the devil. They were a law unto themselves.

Wesley predicted that the result of the belief in predestination (the heart of Calvinism) would result in this antinomianism and lead to the moral decay of the culture. At that time in England, there was only one culture—the Church of England was a state church. Based on what we see happening with so many priests in the Catholic Church today and how the hierarchy seems to try to protect the guilty, I wonder why our culture has, for the most part, based its faith in theology that seems to encourage bad behavior, a theology that I find to be counterintuitive and counter to all of Scripture.

There is a passage in Ezekiel that demands that those who are listening push against the darkness of those who are not listening. Chapter 3:16–27 makes clear the connection between pushing back against the darkness and salvation. God will hold us accountable not only for our obedience but also for confronting those who are disobedient. Pushing back against the darkness is not optional; it's a demand. Ezekiel puts a stumbling block before those evil ones who are not listening.

I believe that the stumbling block is the Jews' inability to listen to Jesus who not only came to save but also to be Lord overall. He remains a stumbling block to those who make Him savior but fails to make Him Lord overall. Belief gets one to judgment, but not through judgment. Calvin did not address the issue of lordship, and it plays no part in his theology. This is a glaring omission and, I believe, a fatal flaw in thinking that belief is the evidence of salvation. Faith in Jesus as Lord is what gets one through Judgment. Simply put, belief gets you to judgment; lordship gets you through judgment.

Nowhere is this more clearly stated than in Matthew 7:21–23: "Not everyone who says to me 'Lord, Lord,' will enter the Kingdom of heaven, but only the one who does the will of the Father in heaven. Many will say to me on that day, 'Lord, Lord, did we not prophesy in your name, and in your name drive out demons and perform many miracles?' Then I will tell them plainly, 'I never knew you. Away from me, you evildoers.'" (Isaiah 64-6)

I now see Jesus as the child of the promise God made to Abraham. He was obedient unto death—born to live, work, and die for the kingdom. I see Paul as a child of that same promise, obedient unto death—reborn to live, work, and die for the kingdom. I see myself as a "wannabe" reborn child of the promise, wanting to be obedient unto death, living, working, and dying for the kingdom.

Peter says something that I think sums up what I have been led to write, "But in your hearts, set apart Christ as Lord. Always be prepared to answer everyone who asks you to give a reason for the hope that you have. But do this with gentleness and respect" (1 Peter 3:15). Also, I think Paul would get an "A" for his answer to this, "...we wait eagerly for our adoption as sons, the redemption of our bodies. For in this hope we (are) saved. But hope that is seen is no hope at all. Who hopes for what he already has? But if we hope for what we do not yet have, we wait for it patiently" (Romans 8:23–25). Living in the very real promise and hope and anticipating an existence that is beyond our wildest dreams.

Jesus says that He has given the keys to the kingdom to Peter and thus the image of Peter and the pearly gates of Heaven. I now see the keys to the kingdom, not in Peter's hands, but Peter's letters. He starts his first letter with "…new birth into a living hope…" and starts his second letter with what I have called, "three days of grace" [promise, response, reward] (2 Peter 1:3–11). Clear instructions on what it takes to enter the kingdom and to be in God's will to give us the keys to the kingdom.

I have a sense of being completely in step with first-century evangelism and completely out of step with twenty-first-century evangelism. Lordship salvation versus checkmark salvation—just a checkmark on one's bucket list. It is clear to me that Peter was much more focused on getting God's elect into the kingdom, not just into the church.

All of the negative publicity that the mainline churches have been getting lately leads me to believe that, without a major shake-up, it won't be long until the Christian culture will no longer exist as a force against evil in this world. Our culture will have descended into the same darkness that the Jews had descended into 2000 years ago.

Paul gives us a very clear understanding of the foundation of his new faith as he begins his letter to Titus. "Paul, a servant of God and an apostle of Jesus Christ for the faith of God's elect and the knowledge of the truth that leads to godliness – faith and knowledge resting on the hope of the eternal life, which God, who does not lie, promised before the beginning of time…" (NIV Prior to 2011)

In Titus 3:3-7, Paul relates the before and after of his conversion. He first paints an ugly picture of himself and the culture of his time. He then paints a beautiful picture of who he had become, a cleaned-up, new creature, having the hope of eternal life. Paul makes his conversion into a wake-up call in Romans 13:11, "…The hour has come for you to wake up from your slumber because our salvation is nearer now than when we first believed." It is time to have another Great Awakening.

EPILOGUE

By now you must know that John Wesley is a hero of mine. He, his brother Charles and some others took on the whole Christian culture in England. I truly hope that what I have written here will become part of another Great Awakening. Also, I have been made aware that others are writing about this very topic and also hoping for the same outcome. Also, I must add that, as well, I feel a great kinship with John Calvin as I think that he believed the Catholic Church of his time did not understand election and he set out to change that. Because they did not understand election, they could not and/or would not comprehend grace.

When Jesus came the Jews were God's elect, His chosen people to the exclusion of all others. Because of the darkness, the Jewish leaders had descended into, their inability to believe excluded them from the kingdom. The Pharisee's saved mindset was a big part of their inability to receive Jesus as Messiah and the Gospel of Grace that He came to deliver. I think this problem has continued and is evident in Calvinistic theology today. Belief is the evidence of election, received by grace, and entitles one to deserve eternal life.

> It is beyond me why anyone would accept the musings of a radical 16th-century Catholic lawyer (Calvin)—all of which were debunked about

50 years later by a Catholic priest (Arminius). I think Paul perfectly describes the darkness that he came out of, the darkness of the Pharisees and the darkness that today's culture is turning to. "At one time we to were foolish, disobedient, deceived and enslaved by all kinds of passions and pleasures. We lived in malice and envy, being hated and hating one another." (Titus 3:3)

Martin Luther wrote about the difficulty he had with understanding grace. Remember, he was a Catholic priest believing that he was God's elect to the exclusion of all others. He writes in his commentary on Galatians "It seems a small matter to mingle Law and Gospel, faith and works, but it creates more mischief than man's brain can conceive. To mix Law and Gospel not only clouds the knowledge of grace, but it also cuts out Christ altogether."

I think that if both Calvin and Wesley could see where the traditions associated with them are today, they would be greatly disappointed. John Wesley felt very strongly that Calvinism would lead to the moral decay of the culture, a decay which is upon us today. John Calvin did not set out to start a tradition that would come to compete with the Catholic Church in the area of the election. Both believed that they were God's elect to the exclusion of all others. A hatred developed between the two, and a lot of blood was shed as both sides believed the other side to be heretics. It is in this debate over inclusion that both sides exclude themselves.

However, one gets to the point of feeling chosen by God— while being God's elect only makes one a candidate for the kingdom. "We know that we have passed from death to life because we love our brothers. Anyone who does not love remains in death. Anyone who hates his brother is a murderer, and you know that no murderer has eternal life in him." (1John 3:14,15)

The focus on sin and salvation in our culture is what has caused the fragmentation of Christ's Church. How one deals with the sins of the past, and the resurrection that is in our future has for the most part, been the focus and the cause of division. I would hope that, after reading this book, you would put aside your beliefs about these issues and focus on the Lordship of Jesus in your day-to-day life. I believe that by doing so, and helping others to do the same, you would have the effect of bringing unity to Christ's Church and make it necessary for believers to both live in, and understand, the grace that saves us.

Focusing on sin and salvation has taken our culture to a place that markets salvation using guilt as motivation. Laying guilt trips on loved ones seldom, if ever, gets the result that is hoped for. How's that work for you—How's that working for our culture? It might bring some into the church but does it bring people into the kingdom? John Wesley described as "vulgar" the notion of salvation as being delivered from hell and delivered to heaven. For him, the presents and gifts of salvation are the deliverance from the desire to sin. Changing focus is easier said than done. Leaving the sacred saved mindset behind is only the beginning. Scripture demands that those who come out of darkness, push back at that same darkness.

The story of Ruth verifies the truth of what I have been led to write. At her conversion, she became an alien in a foreign land. Her choosing to believe, and her difficult journey to the Promised Land, led to her redemption. Her salvation was both a sacred journey and a divine process. "… To him who overcomes, I will give the right to eat from the tree of life, which is in the paradise of God." Rev. 2:7

Finally, can we agree that there was a logjam in the eyes of Jewish culture which held them back from making Jesus Lord of their lives? Paul knew it well and pointed it out in Romans 10. The roadblock to the Jews was their practice of judging people. It was natural for the Jews to assign people to heaven or hell. Such judgment is rather universal today—that we can judge people into heaven or hell because of what we think and who we think we are. This belief leads us into the darkness that is God's elect, whether then or now, entitles us to, "once we die we go straight to heaven."

Here is Paul's address, Paul's full resolve to us: "But the righteousness that is by faith says: Do not say in your heart, Who will ascend into heaven?… or who will descend into the deep?… But what does it say? The word is near you; it is in your mouth and your heart, that is the word of faith that we are proclaiming: That if you confess with your mouth 'Jesus is Lord,' and believe in your heart that God raised him from the dead, you will be saved." Romans 10 6-9 So there it is—Focusing on sin and salvation gets in the way of the Lordship of Jesus Christ. Our salvation is dependent on "being saved" as we serve Jesus, our Lord, and Master.

Do not minimize the impact of Romans 10 on the culture. Like a "bull in a china shop," Paul dismantles—shatters the centerpiece of their faith, namely, God's elect—entitled to the Kingdom and everything that goes with that. Jesus does the same thing with Nicodemus in John 3 which I characterized in my first book as his "salvation status evaporating." Nicodemus was a powerful, influential man of repute and respect yet Jesus tells him firmly, "You must be born again" to a new vision (vs 3). At that, Nicodemus began to understand and the Lordship of Jesus Christ changed his vision and his destiny.

I think it is fair to say that when Jesus comes back in righteousness and judgment, he will be more than a bull in a china shop. He will forever shatter the notion that anyone is entitled to live forever in his kingdom. Like a bull in a china shop, in the spirit of the Wesleys, I believe that God has led me to be the bull that dismantles that same saved mindset of today so that Christians become kingdom builders. Challenging all believers to grow into maturity and an ever-increasing devotion to the Lordship of Jesus Christ.

THE GOSPEL ACCORDING
TO PAUL

It had been hard for me to get past seeing Titus 3:3–7 as only Paul's conversion, but God had so much more for me in this passage. As I try to bring this to a close, I must share what may be the most important point of this book. I now find in this passage the main elements of God's plan of salvation: Redemption from who he used to be; his being recreated in the image of Christ; and with the hope (and promise) of eternal life. Paul, by putting his salvation in his future, conflicts with what is commonly believed in today's Christian culture. I have dealt with this conflicting view throughout this book and now I know why. For hundreds of years, Christian leaders have promoted the darkness out of which Paul came.

This is the darkness of the Pharisees and the darkness that Jesus came to penetrate. Paul would have never preached a gospel that promoted that darkness. In Titus, we find, in a nutshell, the gospel that he preached, the foundation of which was the hope of eternal life. In Galatians we find Paul, very angrily, denouncing any gospel other than the one that he preached. He makes sure that no one misses his point by saying this twice, anyone preaching a gospel other than what he preached will be "eternally condemned".

Don't miss Paul's sarcasm here as he says, "but even if we, or an angel from heaven, should preach a gospel other than the one we preached to you, let him be eternally condemned" (Gal. 1:8).

I have said in this book, and my previous book, that the saved mindset is fatal to all who possess it. This should remove any doubt about what Paul's point is here and the truth of what God was revealing in me—The Gospel According To Paul. Bible translators and commentators have been trying to obscure this truth using verb tenses, omissions—faulty translations, and contextualizing for years. Witness the change in Titus 1:2 NIV 2011.

It is within the last month that God has pressed this out of me while I waited for the publishing wheels to turn. I put this in at the last minute—God was saving the best point for last.

THE RESURRECTION
OF THE PROMISE

THE DREAM COME TRUE

In writing that last chapter in "The Death of the Promise", I felt like I had arrived at the best point and it made a good stopping point. That was in 2019 but with the Covid-19 crisis, it no longer looked like a good stopping point. I tried not to get too political in that book but what seemed to be a good idea then has changed. My heart for the lost in the Church has expanded to a heart for the loss of the American Dream. In a secular world, America has become the promised land. And just like the real Promised Land, everyone wants to be there. The American Dream will be forever lost if the land of opportunity becomes the land of entitlement. So The Resurrection of the Promise is a continuation of The Death of the Promise.

This is a continuing effort to challenge all people to live in the light of the hope and promise of eternal life in the paradise of God. For most, it will require a new foundation of faith - the foundation on which Paul's faith rested - and what should become the foundation of our faith found in the first three verses of Paul's letter to Titus:

"Paul, a servant of God and an apostle of Jesus Christ, for the faith of God's elect and the knowledge of the truth that leads to godliness - faith and knowledge resting on the hope of eternal life, which God, who does not lie, promised before the beginning of time, and at his appointed season he brought his word to light through the preaching entrusted to me by the command of God our savior," (NIV prior to 2011).

It must be noted here that later NIV's omit "godliness - a faith and knowledge resting on" which begins verse two so that it now reads, "godliness - in hope of eternal life." This is a glaring example of how Paul's true faith, and focus on Christ's Second Coming, is being hidden in today's Christian Culture. Messaging is a popular term to describe this practice - modifying the truth to promote an agenda.

Focusing on sin and salvation and what happens when we die needs to be replaced by a focus on hope in The Promise and what happens when Jesus comes back. It is a lordship issue - Jesus does not become Savior until he becomes Lord and Master. This is the difficult - life long journey of obedience and preparation for that glorious Day of Jesus' return - in righteousness and judgment - to fulfill The Promise. This is not only the recurring theme of the whole of Scripture, it is God's plan of salvation.

The most tragic examples of those who miss salvation are those we find at the end of the Sermon On The Mount and the Goats at the end of The Olivate Discourse (Mat. 7, 24 & 25). Both groups refer to Jesus as Lord - are righteous in their own eyes - but are denied and sent away. A culture that promotes the idea that at the moment of belief the keys to the Kingdom are received and at the moment of death the reward of Heaven is achieved is a culture promoting the darkness of the Jews that Jesus came to penetrate.

The foundation on which faith is built is critical to the journey and destination. The moment of conversion or belief is not the end game - it must lead to a decision on what to believe and change who we are and how to live our life. When simply believing becomes the end game for the culture - Satan has won, you see, even Satan believes. Satan's domain is an unbelieving world and a wrong believing Church. The self-righteous, self-absorbed, saved mindset of our culture today is Satan's workshop - the same as it was 2000 years ago.

Jesus addressed this shift in focus very well in Luke 9:23-24 as he connects the decision to follow him with salvation. This passage assumes and does not deal with conversion or belief as he teaches his disciples. Listen to him: Then he said to them all; "If anyone would come after me, he must deny himself and take up his cross daily and follow me. For whoever wants to save his life will lose it, but whoever loses his life for me will save it." This reveals the fatal nature of the saved mind-set and the critically important saving nature of lordship.

THE BLIND SPOT

The most important question one can ask in this age is "Is there an age to come?" When Jesus is about to die, he interacts with a thief who is about to die also. The thief says to Jesus, "Remember me when you come into your kingdom." At that moment, Jesus makes him a promise; the promise of the ages - this is not all there is - there is life after death. "I tell you the truth today, you will be with me in paradise." This is the same promise God made to Abraham 2000 years earlier, that he had the power to raise the dead to new life. This is the central issue in most world religions, what happens when we die? And what must we do to make that promise of paradise come true?

Jesus, very clearly, answers that question when asked, "What must I do to inherit eternal life?" His answer is, "follow me" which is a step beyond mere belief. Paul, the writer of about half of the New Testament, puts all of this together for us in one sentence, "If you belong to Christ, you are Abraham's seed and heirs according to the promise." Gal. 3:29. Followers (disciples) of Jesus are children of The Promise God made to Abraham which is the Blessed Hope. As a Jewish Pharisee, Paul then Saul, believed that he already possessed eternal life. He and his fellow Pharisees had stopped living in The Promise of eternal life and believed they already possessed what was promised.

It is important for us, in understanding Paul's writing, to know that this was a big part of his conversion. For him, becoming a Christ-follower was going from believing he was saved, possessing eternal life - to the hope of receiving what was promised at Christ's Second Coming. Paul's conversion was therefore going from living in the possession of salvation - to living in the hope and promise of salvation. This is a tragic blind spot in the Christian Culture. Bible scholars, translators, and commentators are, for the most part, promoting the darkness of the Pharisees – the darkness out of which Paul came - the saved mind-set.

God through His Holy Spirit has led me to color in that blind spot with pastels of grace. Extending the grace that saves us to all those around us - loving the unloved - forgiving the unforgivable as a response to the hope and promise of eternal life. I hope you can see how God developed the skill for me to put these thoughts on paper. My first book "The Road to Restoration" was not well written as He was leading me to new insights and the understanding of The Gospel According to Paul. I never felt that I had been saved and believe that had a lot to do with God's ability to lead me into the writing of this project.

In John 5, Jesus says in verse 24, "I tell you the truth, whoever hears my word and believes...". In this passage, Jesus is critical of their inability to hear and listen and makes a connection that is just as true today as it was then. Verse 39-40, "You diligently study Scriptures because you think by them you possess eternal life. These are the Scriptures that testify about me, yet you refuse to come to me and have life." Their saved mind-set got in the way of their hearing and listening and, of course, the relationship. In Luke 9, we have the fatal nature of the saved mindset and here we have the reason why.

THE WATCH PARTY

In Romans 8:18-25, Paul describes Christ's Second Coming as a celebration - celebrating the end of pain and suffering - revealing who the sons of God are (the children of God), and waiting patiently in hope for the promise to be fulfilled for those who have won the race. In this passage, Paul reveals his conversion in a very simple and easily understood way, "...who hopes for what he already has?" (verse 24). There is a passage in Hebrews that may summaries the whole of Scripture and invites all people to attend this watch party, "...But now he has appeared once for all at the end of the ages to do away with sin by the sacrifice of himself. Just as man is destined to die once, and after that to face judgment, so Christ was sacrificed once to take away the sins of many people; and he will appear a second time, not to bear sin, but to bring salvation to those who are waiting for him." (Hebrews 9:26-28).

The idea of the Christian Culture participating in a watch party is new to me, but it only makes sense. Jesus led his disciples to believe that he was going to return soon. This would point them in the direction of living their lives in anticipation of that event and have the effect of starting a never-ending watch party - right up to his return. This was their frame of mind as they wrote, preparing themselves and others for that event. This should be our frame of mind also as we read the New Testament looking forward to the soon coming King, and the Day of Salvation.

This had to be the main focus of the First Century Church; anticipating and preparing for that celebration, inviting all to come to join and share in the Blessed Hope. This makes so much sense now and gives me the desire to be part of a church modeling this faith journey. In Luke 21:28, Jesus says, "...stand up and lift up your heads, because your redemption is drawing near.", and Paul says, "And do this (love), understanding the present time. The hour has come for you to wake up from your slumber because our salvation is nearer now than when we first believed." (Romans 13:11). Also, Paul says, "And do not grieve the Holy Spirit of God, with whom you were sealed for the day of redemption." (Eph. 4:30).

In the entire book of Colossians we find Paul's instructions to the Church - to be prepared for Christ's Second Coming - the unblemished Bride of Christ. As a bonus we also find here the Readers Digest version of the Gospel According to Paul, "Once you were alienated from God and were enemies in your minds because of your evil behavior. But now he has reconciled you by Christ's physical body, through death, to present you holy, without blemish and free from accusation (purified) - if you continue in your faith, established and firm, not moved from the hope held out in the gospel." Col. 1:21-23. For a more detailed version, read Titus 3:3-8.

Faith - the sure hope in anticipating Christ's Second Coming is the Key to the Kingdom. When salvation happens whether past, present or future it is not a meaningless technicality to be debated. The "I'm saved and you're not" attitude should be replaced by "I have a hope in a promise, let me share with you my faith in that Gospel of Hope." (Ref. 1Peter 3:15)

Faith in the Gospel of Hope defined Paul's journey as it had a purity of purpose. He had been sealed - purified by The Holy Spirit for The Day of Redemption and, by extension, also the

Church is to be purified and sealed. Christ's work on the Cross was a pure gift that sealed Paul for his journey and which freed him from the sins of the past. This was his passion - the purity of the Church in preparation for Christ's Second Coming. This makes the Day of Salvation as special for God as it is for His New Creatures - Creatures fit - purified and worthy for the Kingdom.

The pure Nard used to anoint Jesus at Bethany made Him God's fragrant offering - purifying the world of sin. I now see in Paul's letter to the Ephesians the importance of God's people having that same purity of purpose and maintaining that desire for sinless purity, in anticipation of Christ's Second Coming - sealed for the Day of Redemption. Christ's First Coming points to this - God setting the table for that great wedding celebration and banquet when Christ and His Church (Heaven and Earth) are brought together - united on that great getting up morning - The Day of Salvation. "Everyone who has this hope in Him (His appearing) purifies himself, just as He is pure." 1John 3:3.

The anointing of Christ's Body at Bethany foreshadows the anointing of The Church - the purification of the Body of Christ in anticipation of His Second Coming. "BE IMITATORS of God, therefore, as dearly loved children and live a life of love, just as Christ loved us and gave Himself up for us as a fragrant offering and sacrifice to God. But among you there must not be even a hint of sexual immorality, or any kind of impurity, or of greed, because these are improper for God's holy people. ...For of this you can be sure: No immoral, impure or greedy person...has any inheritance in the kingdom of Christ and of God. Let no one deceive you with empty words, for because of such things God's wrath comes on those who are disobedient." Eph 5:1-6.

The Romans used the threat of the cross to purify the minds of those they conquered. Obedience to Roman law was the goal and the cross was the means. This horrible means of punishment now symbolizes God's grace, purification from sin and obedience to the law of love. The Roman cross foreshadows Jesus' return to judge the living and the dead. The weeping and gnashing of teeth at this event are symbolic of God's wrath and the horrible second death.

And again, "For I am already being poured out like a drink offering, and the time has come for my departure. I have fought the good fight, I have finished the race, I have kept the faith (sure hope). Now there is in store for me the crown of righteousness, which the Lord, the righteous judge, will award to me on that day (Day) - not only to me, but also to all who have longed for His appearing." 2Tim 4:6-8. Focusing on the awarding of salvation at the moment of belief is a death march. Focusing on the awarding of salvation resulting from purification (lordship and obedience) - leads to life. "For whoever wants to save his life will lose it, but whoever will lose his life for me will save it." Luke 9:24.

Shifting focus from The Second Coming to what happens when they died would have demonstrated a complete lack of faith of those in The First Century Church. Their faith, trust and belief would have been completely tied to Jesus fulfilling The Promise at His return. The definition of faith in the first century was therefore faith in Jesus "...to bring salvation to those who are waiting on Him" - being sure of what was hoped for. Since most, if not all, in The Twenty First Century Church believe that they have already received and possess salvation, the question begs to ask, what is the definition of their faith and their hope?

The above quote is from Heb. 9:28. When I read this verse in a word for word translation from Greek to English (The Pure Word), I find God's plan of salvation in a nutshell. Jesus came once to purify the whole world - the many. His teaching and His Holy Spirit guide the few into purity a of purpose and purity of life leading to salvation. "So Christ was once made offered to Bear Up as in an Offering for the sin nature and sins of many. A Second

Time He shall Spiritually Appear to those without sin nature and sin Waiting for Salvation." The Pure Word.

The observation that today's Church bears little resemblance to The First Century Church has been made by others. One commentator, that I read, made the same comment about The Eleventh Century Church. So many things have been written about faith and what to believe, how can anyone know what true faith and belief are? We must try to uncomplicate what has become so complicated. And he said, "I tell you the truth unless you change and become like little children, you will never enter the kingdom of heaven." (Mat. 18:3) The definition of faith found in Hebrews 11:1 is so simple even a child can understand it, why have we made it so complicated? "Now faith is being sure of what is hoped for certain of what we do not (yet) see."

What does not make sense is; thinking that we can capture our children and young adults with a focus on what happens when we die. When that becomes our focus, we become a Church for older adults (seniors). Young people are mostly focused on life and living, not on death and dying. This has become a fatal flaw in today's Church. When we focus on Christ's Second Coming, we will take advantage of this lack of concern of death and dying and build on the 'never die' mystique and how Jesus makes this come true at His Second Coming.

Millennials want America to become a kinder and gentler nation and have been led to believe the Church is a part of the problem. It is easy to see why. An "I'm saved and you're not" attitude sends an "I'm going to Heaven when I die and you're going to hell when you die" message. This must change. We have met the enemy and he is us. Paul very clearly says we are not to assign people to heaven or hell.

A lot of my theological beliefs line up with John Wesley's and Arminian thought which means that Calvin was wrong. John Calvin was a French Catholic lawyer who believed that God chose winners and losers. From the beginning of time, a person was chosen by God to believe and receive salvation - all others were excluded. Christ's work on the Cross was limited to certain people - God's unconditionally elect. The debate between the Catholic Church and the Calvinists (each one believing they were saved to the exclusion of all others) erupted into an all-out war; a war that lasted about 100 years, 1550-1650.

It is estimated that 8,000,000 people died in Europe as a result of this war over "I'm saved and you're not". Now you know the main reason why Christians were willing to risk their lives to escape Europe and come to the New World. This debate lasted into our lifetime. I have friends who were taught as children - Baptists were saved to the exclusion of all others - Catholics were saved to the exclusion of all others. It is worth noting that the reformer Martin Luther and John Calvin were contemporaries but were not on the same page. Luther had a problem with the marketing of salvation - the Catholic Church selling indulgences, buying one's way into heaven.

In Paul's letter to the Galatians, he is upset with them over preaching a competing gospel. Could it be that they were already promoting the darkness of the Pharisees, the darkness out of which he came, and reinventing that darkness for future generations which leads to eternal condemnation or being accursed? God, through Paul, was already dealing with the blind spot. Paul highlights the main points of his Gospel in Titus 3:3-8: at conversion he was saved from who he was as a Pharisee, he was reborn - conformed to the image of Christ and lived the rest of his life in the hope and promise of eternal life.

In Hebrews 11, we find the icing on the cake for this idea of a watch party. This chapter is often referred to as the faith hall of fame. It starts with, "Now faith is being sure of what we hope for and certain of what we do not see." It ends by bringing all people of faith, both old and new, into the moment of reward and celebration planned by God. "These were all commended for their faith, yet none of them received what had been promised. God had planned something better for us so that only together with us would they be made perfect." Without a doubt, God is saving the best for last.

When viewed in this way, there is perfect symmetry. Jesus' first miracle foreshadows his last miracle - turning water into wine at the wedding party in Cana - and Jesus coming for his bride at another wedding party (banquet) and his last miracle at the resurrection. God's plan of salvation is planning for a wedding party - a party for the ages. In Mathew 25, we find three parables that help us understand what happens at His Second Coming. These are stories of inclusion and exclusion. "The Parable of the Ten Virgins" perfectly describes our need to live in excited expectation of this wedding banquet and the arrival of the bridegroom. The story also describes the consequences of not doing so - a tragic consequence for the five foolish young ladies at the very last minute.

Jesus could make his point here without using young ladies as an example. There is a deeper point here - these young ladies were a product of guidance they received at home and in their culture, some wise and some foolish. Is our generation just the last in a long line passing on the false hope of eternal security gained at conversion? Let us not make this about our generation or previous generations - let's make it about the next generation. This is where my heart is. This is a story of accountability - no grace - no mercy - only justice. We will likewise be held accountable.

Here, Jesus paints a very black and white picture of the Day of Judgement with no gray areas. It is important in looking forward to the judgment that we keep in mind the simple definition of three words - justice, mercy, and grace. Justice is getting what you deserve; mercy is not getting what you deserve; grace is getting more than you deserve. Let us hope we never reach a point on our journey where we are deserving of receiving the grace that saves us. Let us look forward to the moment when Jesus says to each of us, "well done thou good and faithful servant.", our moment of inclusion.

We have a choice between a gospel that looks forward to what happens at Christ's Second Coming when the promise of salvation and resurrection will be fulfilled - or a gospel that looks forward to what happens when we die believing the promises of salvation and resurrection have been completely fulfilled at Easter. Burying the hatchet in the war over "I'm saved and you're not" and just focusing on believe and be saved is not the answer. The answer is living grace-filled lives where Jesus is truly Lord and sharing with others our hope in The Promise that is yet to be fulfilled.

I don't believe there is a clearer understanding of the phrase, "saved by grace through faith" than the following - "Therefore, with minds that are alert and fully sober, set your hope on the grace to be brought to you when Jesus Christ is revealed at His coming." (1 Peter 1:13). Jesus is the messenger, the deliverer of The Promise and therefore, Peter's faith is in The Promise more than the person, the faith of Abraham.

THE PROPHECY

John Wesley predicted that theology based on predestination (Calvinism) would lead to the moral decay of the culture. At the time of his prediction, there was only one culture in England - the church culture which was fundamentally Calvinist. As a young man, he came to America but was ineffective in ministry here. He went back to England and God used him in a mighty way. It is hard to say how man's efforts and God's plan work together but it is safe to say that John Wesley's work in England played a large part in The Great Awakening.

Part of his prediction was that the culture would become a law unto itself or eventually become lawless. Antinomianism is the term that describes this moral decay. When we see what is going on in America today, we can see his prediction has come true or at least is coming true. The Church is just as much to blame as the "inside the beltway crowd" for the unrest in the streets of some of our cities. There is an awful lot to debate here as to where the blame lies but most of the blame lies in our institutions of higher learning. Many of these institutions were founded to promote Christianity and train preachers. After taking God out of our public schools, they have become, for the most part, Godless institutions. In John Wesley's opinion, these institutions of his time would have done well to teach priest candidates to be Christian before they were taught to be priests – Godless institution training Christian leaders.

John Wesley's prediction of moral decay and lawlessness was made around the time of our revolutionary war. Getting away from English rule was also getting away from the English church-state which came with being English Colonies. It is not a stretch to believe the freedom of religion we enjoy today grew out of a desire, in some, to be free of the Church of England. Our founding fathers were men who loved God - one of which said that this government would only work for a moral people. The love of money - and immoral behavior - seem to have replaced the love of God and the morality that goes with that love. The theology of the Church of England has had a great influence on what is being taught our seminaries today. John Wesley, a man of God, saw this coming and made this connection in his time. Today's Church leaders, some of whom might be Christian in name only, must be blind not to see and make this connection in our time.

I have experienced this blindness both in the local Church and in seminary - two of my children are seminarians. It is believed and being taught that John Wesley and John Calvin agreed and that Jacabus Armenius and John Calvin agreed also. Nothing could be further from the truth. This is another blind spot generated by wrong belief or in this case, a lie right straight out of hell. TULIP is an acronym developed by later Calvinists to counter Armineus's five points of disagreement with Calvin's theology. The acronym TULIP and Armenian thought exist only because of the disagreement.

Instead of another great awakening, there is happening today a great falling away. We hear it in sermons and we see it happening around us in friends and family. The tension in our politics today seems mostly about moving from being a land of opportunity to become a land of entitlement. The story of the prodigal speaks loudly to this debate. The younger son asked his father to give him that to which he was entitled. He wanted to possess what was promised, his inheritance. When his father's money ran out he came to his senses and returned home. He had left the land of entitlement and returned to the land of opportunity - a chance to redeem himself. To begin with, the young man felt he had a right to his inheritance. It was there for the taking. Our eternal reward is often referred to as an inheritance in Scripture.

This lawlessness that John Wesley predicted is getting worse. At the heart of this attitude is feeling entitled to anything that has not been earned. The rioting and looting today has people and businesses fleeing these large cities with no end in sight. I open this can of worms to say that the entitlement mentality inside the Church, being taught in our seminaries, has moved into the culture in a very ugly way. As the Church goes, so goes the culture. The moment of belief has become the moment of entitlement.

Fleeing blue states and moving to red states has been going on for a long time. Virginia is a good example of that transition. There used to be a balance here, but that is no longer the case. For the most part, Virginia is now a blue state. Those who fled blue states for a better way of life brought their politics with them. Virginia is moving from a land of opportunity to a land of entitlement. Politics and the spread of the Covid-19 virus seem to have a lot in common.

A great falling away can be seen as a departure from true faith. Peter addresses his concern about this in 1 Peter 1:7, "These (griefs and trials) have come so that your faith ... may be proved genuine...". Faith without understanding becomes just a word and loses its true meaning. It is important to understand and it is not complicated - it is the faith in Jesus to deliver what God promised to Abraham and, by extension, promised to us. A child of faith is a child of hope and a child of The Promise.

After identifying competing gospels in "The Death of the Promise", it follows that there must be competing faiths. One must follow the other and is inescapable. One faith demands preparation and anticipation - the other demands nothing but belief. One is a watch party gospel that demands not only preparation, it demands pushing against the darkness. The other is a pew potato gospel with no demands, just "easy believism" and "cheap grace". Paul's conversion demonstrates the continuing demands of pushing against the darkness. His new faith demanded that he push against the darkness, out of which he came, for the rest of his life.

The assurance that we sing about and hear about in so many sermons is available to the believer. But that belief must lead to genuine faith. This is a faith that grows out of adversity. Not so much the adversities of our natural life, but the adversities of our spiritual life - pushing against the darkness of wrong belief in ourselves and others. This wrong belief must be overcome to get to where assurance awaits. This was Jesus' mission; this was Paul's mission and it must become the mission of today's disciples - pushing against the darkness of the Pharisees - the saved mindset.

THE UNITY OF THE FAITH

"There is one body and one Spirit - just as you were called to one hope when you were called - one Lord, one faith, one baptism; one God and father of all, who is over all and through all and in all." (Eph. 4:4-6). This is part of the passage where Paul is calling all workers in the faith to reach for unity in the faith. This is not the unity of belief - belief is assumed here. There is no wiggle room here, one hope and one faith are, in Paul's world, focused on the Second Coming. This has not changed and should be the common goal of church leaders which Paul points out here. Right in the middle of the faith hall of fame, we find a call to action tied to faith and belief. "And without faith, it is impossible to please God, because anyone who comes to him must believe that he exists and that he rewards (he is the Rewarder of - Amplified) those who earnestly seek him." (Heb. 11:6) Faith is a journey from belief to the reward of The Promise being fulfilled.

Faith has an element of individuality not unlike our physical DNA and family markers. Each person's faith is unique but has family markers also. Unlike our physical DNA that never changes, our spiritual DNA changes as we grow. The family markers of spiritual DNA are the things we hold in common with other like-minded individuals. Paul's spiritual DNA changed dramatically after his encounter with Jesus on the road to Damascus. Paul had to be a Pharisee so that we can see this radical change - going from the possession of salvation to the hope of salvation. This is a very important family marker of our spiritual DNA.

From the beginning of his first letter to the end of his second letter, Peter sets up these family markers. Phrase after phrase, sentence after sentence, he puts his spiritual DNA on display. It is so compact and straightforward and understandable that there is no room for error just like physical DNA. From his first thought to his last he gives us our family markers. "...In his great mercy, he has given us new birth into a living hope..." (1Peter 1:3) - to the last paragraph of 2 Peter, "...be on your guard so that you may not be carried away by the error of lawless men and fall from your secure position. But grow in the grace and knowledge of our Lord and Savior Jesus Christ. To him be glory both now and forevermore."

When Peter says that Paul's writings are hard to understand and then identifies them as Scripture, a spiritual tag team match comes into view. God, through The Holy Spirit, promoting a fight against the forces of evil with his chosen team. Paul, the preacher, and Peter the layman, leading the way in the battle against the darkness. God's guidance shows through, it seems, as Peter may be trying to bring a layman's understanding of what was difficult for him to understand in Paul's writing. A family DNA marker emerges that is inescapable. Fighting against the darkness is in the DNA of the writers of the New Testament and by extension must be in ours also.

The passage, beginning at Ephesians (4:3), is very important to help understand the work of The Holy Spirit in the pursuit of genuine faith. "Make every effort to keep the unity of the Spirit... until we all reach unity in the faith and the knowledge of the Son of God and become mature, attaining to the whole measure of the fullness of Christ." (Eph. 4:13). Paul's point here seems to be that the Spirit who calls us to one hope, will bring God's people to one faith as defined in Hebrews 11:1. Paul is not splitting hairs here, this is important, he is teaching us about the faith that, not only saves us - but that same faith will unify us. This is another important marker in our family DNA.

Jesus puts some of the elements in Luke 9:23-24; in Luke 14 25-33. This is where Jesus teaches about the cost of discipleship. He uses two examples: one is to have the resources to complete building a tower and second: to have the resources to win a battle with a stronger foe. He ends this passage by saying, "In the same way, any of you who does not give up everything he has cannot be my disciple." (verse 33). Reading these two passages in Luke together will help bring into focus the family DNA of a disciple; living and winning at all costs.

THE CRISIS

The Covid-19 pandemic has brought to the fore the insecurity of life in this world. We want a vaccine and we want it now. This is evidence of why eternal security is marketed in our Churches today, just as it was in the Temple when Jesus came. We want eternal security in this world as well as the next. One of our founding fathers said something like this, "Anyone who would give up their freedom to gain security deserves neither." The tension between security and freedom has always been with us.

All this has to do with wanting a utopian existence in this world as well as the next. The idea that man can create this utopia through his own efforts in this world came into its own about the same time that Calvin was making his pitch for eternal security in the next world. At the same time, Luther was rebelling against marketing security in the next world by selling indulgences in the Catholic Chuch. All three of these movements had at their core man's desire for security whether now or in the future. Jesus came to set us free from the fear of death and dying and yet man seems to be forever enslaved by it.

Calvin's theology came with no price tag. Man had the freedom to continue to live his life as he pleased. Also, whether we give our wealth to the Church or the poor, they both can have the element of purchasing salvation. This is why Jesus' interaction with the rich (young) ruler must be read as hyperbole, illustrating absurdity using absurdity. "Follow me", is the instruction and lordship is the answer to the question, "What must I do to inherit eternal life?".

Being enslaved by our fear of death is brought out by the writer of Hebrews. "Since the children have flesh and blood, he to shared in their humanity so that by his death he might destroy him who holds the power of death - that is, the devil - and free those who all their lives were held in slavery by their fear of death." (Heb. 2:13-14). This makes it abundantly clear that today's debate and tension is a spiritual war between security and freedom and fear is a powerful weapon. Choosing freedom from the fear of death is where security awaits and that is the freedom and security that Jesus offers. "The fear of the Lord is the beginning of wisdom.", while the fear of dying is a death march.

The story of the prodigal has an important element of freedom - the freedom to fail. In giving his son his inheritance, the father gave him the freedom to fail. In welcoming him home, the son was given the freedom to succeed. That is the freedom we have in America as it is now but will not exist in a socialist America. Investing the wealth generated by the freedom to succeed is what has made America the richest country in the world. As America goes, so goes the world. Taking that wealth away from the successful and giving it to the unsuccessful will destroy the American way of life and equality will be achieved through poverty.

In our lifetime a book was published titled, "Rules for Radicals" written by Saul Alinski. In this book, you will find a blueprint for what is going on in America today. Written by a community organizer, you will find a socialist agenda, a plan to collapse the economy, and the marching orders to never let a crisis go the waist and much more. It should be no surprise that in their younger days both Barak Obama and Hillary Clinton worked closely with this man. You can be sure that they, along with Bernie Sanders, are doing everything they can to promote Joe Biden and their socialist agenda. The code word for this agenda is progressive.

The crash on Wall Street gave us Social Security. Like most social programs, they look good at first but socialists are seldom done. The Social Security "lockbox" had no lock on it and now what comes in, soon goes out. I am on Social Security and I do not receive the money I put in. I receive what my children and grandchildren put in. Politicians in Washington have turned a worthwhile program into a Ponzi scheme. This would not be so bad if I didn't know their end game. Saul Alinski let the cat out of the bag about fifty years ago and socialist Bernie Sanders has let the cat loose again and let everyone know what their end game is.

I touched on some of this in "The Death of the Promise" but, at that time, I could not see what was coming. I hinted at the liberal political/Christian connection but it now seems very important to write about the obvious similarities between the entitlement mindset in both cultures. Maybe we have digressed into the one culture from which our forefathers tried to escape. A spiritual war is not a war that can be won on this earth. Satan is always at work using fear of death to enslave man. Christ's victory over sin on Friday evening and His victory over death Sunday morning set up a never-ending war with darkness. This war lies between our conversion and our resurrection at His return. Remember, it is in our family spiritual DNA to push against the darkness. Jesus did not win this victory on the Cross, He gave us hope to fight and to win a war that has been going on since the Garder of Eden. This war will be won in the final victory when He comes back. I am thankful that He gives us a chance to be victorious in small measure in this present life.

THE WIDE AND
NARROW ROADS

The road to restoration is a good description of the journey from paradise destroyed to paradise restored. "Enter through the narrow gate. For wide is the gate and broad is the road that leads to destruction, and many enter through it. But small is the gate and narrow the road that leads to life, and only a few find it." (Matt. 7:13-14). That first step is so important to the destination. There always will be missteps along the way but do not make that first step, a misstep. The idea that the moment of belief is the moment of salvation is such a wide gate that once on the broad road the many will never consider their first step to being a misstep.

The wide appeal of entitlement in today's American Culture is evident inside and outside the Church. Jesus follows this passage with a warning, "Watch out for false prophets. They come to you in sheep's clothing, but inwardly they are ferocious wolves." (verse 15). This description fits today's politics perfectly. Things are going on in America today that need watching.

The socialist will admit their vision for America will cost a lot of money. At first, they will tax rich corporations. This money will be used to attract illegals with the promise of free everything including free legal advice on becoming legal residents and voters.

They have already outlined this plan but they will need more money because they are never through. The next thing they will do is come after the money in our retirement accounts, our 401K's and IRA"s. This idea was floated in the Clinton years but got nowhere at that time. They will do all of this a quickly as they can, in hope of causing our economy to collapse which they will blame on the previous administration. We got a taste of this when so much of our economy was shut down due to Covid-19.

What follows is anybody's guess, but the war on wealth, both in the streets of our cities and in Washington D.C., will continue. They will never quit because socialist leaders always escape the poverty (food deserts) they cause. Wolves in sheep's clothing, devouring our wealth and spending this ill-gotten wealth on themselves. We have a good example of this in Hunter Biden.

The battle lines are as clear now as they have ever been and no matter who wins in November, the socialist, communist, Marxist agenda will never go away. Satellite imagery shows the darkness in North Korea compared to South Korea. This is a dramatic example contrasting the land of opportunity with the land of entitlement, each pushing against the other until Jesus comes back. He will reward his servants with the final victory and a second birth and His foes with a defeat and a second death.

Jesus ends his teaching ministry in Matthew with the three parables in Chapter 25. We have already looked at "The Ten Virgins", now let's look at the other two. The story of the talents is a story of building wealth. A talent represented a lot of money - somewhere in the millions or even billions of dollars. But who's counting?

The master leaves his servants in charge of his wealth. His servants take it upon themselves to increase his fortune while he is away. The exception is the one talent servant. This servant does not put the money to work, instead, he buries it for safekeeping.

"You wicked, lazy (slothful) servant... throw that worthless servant outside, into the darkness, where there will be weeping and gnashing of teeth." (Verses 28-30).

The best explanation I have heard of this last phrase is; the weeping is because of their disappointment, the gnashing of teeth is anger over being clueless and anger with those who kept them in the dark. In this story, there is a contrast between freedom and security. Choosing the freedom to pursue wealth and by comparison choosing, poverty found in security.

Sloth is one of the seven deadly sins as illustrated here. A life of leisure has become the main goal and the American dream. Retirement from chasing that almighty dollar - to a life of other pursuits has replaced a life that is forever acquiring financial security. It is preached today that God wants us to be happy. He did come to clean-up our mess, but only through obedience does that happen. This parable connects happiness with increasing the wealth of the master; "Come and share in your master's happiness." Our founding Fathers debated over the phrase, "the pursuit of happiness", some wanted "the pursuit of personal property", which of course was the pursuit of wealth. It just sounded better.

Happiness is not in retirement - happiness is in finding new and better ways to serve. There is a focus in these last two parables on what one must do for God which is different than the focus on what God has done for us. There is also no element of instruction, only justice, and consequences. If there is instruction, it lies in the consequences.

In "The Sheep and the Goats", Jesus starts by making it a parable of inclusion and exclusion in His Kingdom. Until, He separates the sheep from the goats, they have no clue there is a difference. To begin with, the sheep seem to be clueless about why Jesus has separated them for special treatment and a good reward. At the end of the parable, the goats seem to be clueless about what they did wrong and are crushed by their reward. This story has the element of looking back over a life of service which both groups had.

Verse 32 "All the nations will be gathered before him, and he will separate the people one from another as a shepherd separates the sheep from the goats." The word nations here refer to ethnic groups. At that time these groups would have had their own spiritual identity. Thus it would be better understood today as denominational groups, each one having their own spiritual identity. This was separating nations, not on the physical DNA we find in ethnic groups, but on spiritual DNA found in denominational beliefs. Getting rid of denominational identities does not get rid of the family markers of spiritual DNA.

There is an element that is unspoken here but must be considered; the heartbreak of Jesus telling those goats of their plight. They are the "I never knew you" crowd at the end of "The Sermon on the Mount". Those who were warned about their sand foundation and like the Pharisees had their heads buried in the sand of believing they were already saved. That heartbreak has to be shared by the sheep, "We didn't know". This is about the community of believers being separated into two groups at Christ's return.

There is no clear difference between the two groups. Some might say that motivation was the difference. James says, "Faith without works is dead", so faith and works must work together to save us. The two groups having two different faiths have to be the problem here. One group received grace and was saved, the other group did not receive grace and was excluded.

This is heartbreaking for those sheep who have genuine faith and have been in community with the goats who have a faith that did not save them. The lesson here is for all believers to focus on genuine faith and avoid the heartbreak that will be at Christ's return. This parable has puzzled me for thirty years and I thank God for helping me now to understand the problem and alert fellow believers, that belief is not the end game. It's the first step of a faith journey with the sure hope that leads to everlasting life.

When believers bring a saved mindset to Matthew 25 and thus to judgment, there is little or nothing to be learned here. These believers are found sheep and they do not find themselves here. Paul understood the critical nature of the unity of faith and now we can see how Jesus, teaching about works - deeds of service, makes this the most important point. Without Jesus mentioning faith, we can see the faith that saves is the faith that we carry to judgment in anticipation of receiving God's saving grace. It is the faith of the First Century Church. Genuine faith, works of service, and God's saving grace work together to save - nothing more - nothing less.

It is important to note here that in Ephesians 2:8-10, Paul says this - "For by grace you have been saved through faith - and this not of your own selves, it is the gift of God - not by works so that no one can boast. For we are God's workmanship, created in Christ Jesus to do good works, which God prepared in advance for us to do." Paul would have never used the past tense, "have been saved through faith" - instead he would have said - "will be saved through faith". This is pivotal in understanding the Gospel and how grace, genuine faith and works of service come together to make The Promise come true.

Works are not unto salvation, they are an outgroath of a faith that leads to salvation. This goes with James saying, "Faith without works is dead." Changing the verb tense here makes it clear that genuine faith is in God The Father sending His Son as the Messenger - Deliverer of what God promised to Abraham - everlasting life to those who have been preparing and are waiting on this event and thus their salvation.

It is fair to say that Paul reveals his Good News Gospel that leads to life and a competing bad news gospel that leads to death. Those who promote salvation at convertion and going to heaven at the moment of death have created a Good News blackout. Paul pushed against this darkness, the darkness out of which he came - a darkness that has persisted through the ages to today. World-wide evangelism seems to be focused on recieving salvation at the moment of belief and going to heaven at the moment of death both of which are contrairy to what Paul preached. (Ref. Eph. 2:8-10 & James 2:14-26)

> "By salvation, I mean not... the vulgar notion
> (of) deliverance from hell or going to heaven but
> a present deliverance from (the desire to) sin. the
> renewal of our souls after the image of God in
> righteousness and true holiness, in justice, mercy,
> and truth."
>
> John Wesley -1745-

THE PROMISE

God's plan of salvation is very much a plan to restore the relationship that was broken in the Garden of Eden by disobedience and the desire to sin. At our conversion, that desire to sin will erupt into a civil war within that new believer. The battle between our flesh and God's Spirit begins at our conversion and ends at our death. When Christ comes in righteousness and judgment, he also comes to restore - to mend - that broken relationship. It is a moment that all who are saved by grace through faith will be made perfect and be restored to paradise. Salvation is God's business, not ours. Developing and having a genuine faith is our business - a faith that focuses on being prepared for what happens when Jesus appears.

The faith of the Jewish people was very much tied to their birthright. One could adopt the Jewish faith but the only way to be Jewish was to be born of a Jewish mother. In our physical DNA there is a part that is passed on from mother to child that never changes. There is also a part that is passed on from father to son that also never changes. I find this interesting in that these two elements are very present in the Jewish faith. Their faith rested on birthright, Abraham's blood running through their veins, the blood sacrifice and obedience to The Law. God's loving kindness (grace) plus faith, plus works made one right with God and was their birthright. This is very similar to what I have found in New Testament Scripture: God's saving grace, plus genuine faith, plus works, leads to a born again birthright and The Promise of eternal life.

About the time of the Bible being assembled, a concept appeard that we were "saved by grace alone". This concept has come down through the ages and is alive in the Christian Culture today. I have been told this concept comes out of Paul's letter to the Galatians. A letter in which he warns of a gospel other than the one he preached - a flawed gospel that led to eternal condemnation. I can not find this "grace alone" concept in Galatians. Instead, in Galatians, I find an emphasis on faith in a promise God made to Abraham. In chapter 2, Paul emphasizes that we are "justified by faith". So much so that at the end of the chapter, in verse 21, he feels he must say this, "I do not set aside (nullify) the grace of God..."

In chapter 5, he lists practices that will exclude believers from the Kingdom and practices that will include believers in the Kingdom. This makes the concept of "saved by grace alone" very flawed and brings to light Paul's view of salvation: grace, plus faith, plus works, saves. Might Paul be dealing with that flawed concept already? He wrote Galatians near the end of his life and seems to want to counter a growing emphasis on the fallacy of "grace alone". He also may be dealing with Jews making Jesus just a nice addition to what they already believed. The teachers of The Law and Pharisees already believed they possessed eternal life. Conversion would be easier if they brought that belief with them and left behind the blood sacrifice and obedience to The Law - paving a very broad road to salvation.

Peter uses most of his second letter warning about this practice of distorting Paul's letters. Near the end, he has this warning, "Bear in mind that our Lord's patience means salvation, just as our dear brother Paul also wrote you with the wisdom that God gave him. He writes the same way in all his letters, speaking in them of these matters. His letters contain some things that are hard to understand, which ignorant and unstable people distort, as they do with other Scriptures, to their own destruction", Second Peter 3:15-16. Patience in waiting on salvation at the end of the journey versus the instant gratification of receiving salvation at the beginning. Pick one.

As I bring this to a conclusion the hearings on the Supreme Court nominee are going on. The debate seems to be between those who want a narrow view of our Constitution (our gospel) and those who want a broad view. Leaders in government and leaders in The Church are, in effect, trying to re-unite church and state on the broad road. In both cultures this is the road that leads to death and destruction. Two separate and distinct gospels, but together uniting church and state.

THE RED SCARE 20/20

In the 1920's, after World War I, Americans were in a time where many were afraid of what had happened in Russia and of worldwide communist aggression. This feeling was labeled "The Red Scare". I believe many in America are experiencing another red scare today. I am a Christian who lives the faith of the First Century Church, simply stated, I live in anticipation of receiving an eternal reward when Christ returns bringing salvation to those who are waiting on Him - as I look up, my redemption draws near.

I have always felt that I was born in a very interesting time (1944) - three months before my father fought in the "Battle of the Bulge". As a teenager, he shared something that has stuck with me - as they returned home, he and many of his fellow soldiers felt America had allied with our true enemy (Russia) in order to win the war. A generation later, I was the right age to go to war against Communist aggression in South East Asia. I volunteered to escape the draft with a European commitment and was trained and assigned to keep an eye on the Russian Army in East Germany. I was in a cold war in Germany while others were in a hot war on the other side of the world. It was a flesh and blood war where body counts were reported daily. In reality it was a spiritual war between the godlessness of Karl Marx and a country founded on

Old Testament principles and the worship of the God of Abraham, Isaac and Jacob.

I decided to write about how I see parallels in my spiritual life and my life lived in this Land of Opportunity. I have already shared much of my views on this but needed to look back on how I have experienced this war with Communism. There are several things that jump out at me from my teen years. There was a Senator on TV named Joe McCarthy and an Un-American Activities Committee that seemed rather unhinged focusing on the advance of Communism in America. There was a TV series "I Led Three Lives" about the adventures of a Russian double agent in America which my dad never missed. There was Sputnik and a space race that began in the early 60's. We had to beat the Russians to the Moon. In the eighth grade George Orwell's "1984" and "Animal Farm" were required reading. Then there was the beginning of a real war in Vietnam with the communists in 1965.

I hit 20 needed a change of scenery and was looking at being drafted. My number came up while I was on leave after basic training - the troop buildup began in earnest while I was in basic as I was about to turn 21 with my European commitment. In July, four years later, I watched the Moon Landing and a few weeks later came home from Germany. I came home to an America that was in turmoil - the rioting in Watts and our troops being spit on as they came home from Vietnam.

I realize now that I had lived my life without worrying about what was happening in distant places. What seemed at the time just news stories, has become for me a continuum of events leading up to today's turmoil and those who advocate for a socialist - Marxist agenda and country. It is apparent today that many on the west coast believed we were fighting the wrong enemy in Vietnam. Their enemy was a government warring against communism - a system they embraced. Spiting on our returning troops was their way of spiting on Washington D.C. and by extension, our Constitution.

The venom against our President and all things Trump is nothing new - just a new generation spiting on a government that they despise. The news blackouts on anything that hurts their cause, and anything that helps the constitutionalist, is remarkable and obvious. In the same way, the "Deep State" seems to be doing the same thing. The socialist attempt to deceive voters with misinformation about Russian collusion in the last election (LOL) and three years of searching for a reason to impeach is true to their agenda. It would be totally out of form for them not to try to steal this election. The banana republic methodology was ideal for this time of the Covid-19 scare. Jane Fonda (Hanoi Jane) has recently made a similar point about this opportunity.

I have made the point of The Christian Church promoting the darkness out of which Paul came. Now I will make the point of America returning to the darkness out of which we came. In order to do this, I have to believe that our founders were already enjoying the American Dream and the Land of Opportunity. In order to assure that this would continue they needed to break with England. The elements of our founding documents were taking form in their hearts and minds as they enjoyed this new found freedom. They did not embark on a new journey - they were just securing the journey they were already on. I think it is fair to say that this journey was a journey from the darkness of a very controlling king and government to a less controlling government with no king.

Ronald Reagan warned us about how government control of health care would take our freedom away from us which is now in the process of coming true. It is a giant step in the return to the darkness out of which we came. When the government controls our health care - the government controls us. The tyranny of socialism always has a "Big Brother" who calls the shots. The flag of Virginia has a picture of a dead tyrant representing the King of England with the caption "Thus Unto Tyrants". The state of Virginia has in this election voted for the tyranny represented on our flag. All of our state wide elected offices are held by democrats supporting this socialist agenda.

It is ironic that Joe Biden's political career has spanned the time of our war on communism in Vietnam which, as a democrat, he probably supported - to a party supporting those who would fundamentally change our republic into another version of North Vietnam. This is nothing new for the Democrat Party. Our Declaration of Independence was written in part to do away with slavery. Georgia declined to go along with that language and it was deleted. This was the foundation of the solid south Democrat Party - the party of slavery and ultimately the party of division. The first Republican President came to the rescue to preserve the Union and took the opportunity to right a wrong that had threatened to defeat us before we even got started.

I see the party of Abraham Lincoln continuing to be the party wanting to solve problems and preserve this union as it was founded - while I see the Democrat Party having a long history of creating problems and then promising to fix them. They seem to derive their power from the problems with no evidence of wanting a solution. Most of the problems today seem to come from those who want to dismantle our Constitution. Has anybody noticed that the heir apparent to Joe Biden's throne hails from the sanctuary city by the bay.

At this moment of time there has been one man standing in the way of this present war on our Constitution and I believe we have a picture that defines this moment in history. God's fingerprints are all over the picture of our President starkly standing alone in front of a church clutching a Bible which angered those he stood against - (God uses who He chooses). This moment and the reaction that followed reveals and defines today's division in our country to a "T". In the days leading up to the election we saw on TV the hatred on one side building to a fevered pitch. At the same time all over America we saw mega rallies chanting "We Love You" to our President. Love of our President and our Constitution defining one side - despising our President and voting for those who would dismantle our Constitution defining the other.

The Bible makes clear that God's people will be defined by love; love of our fellow man, love of God, love of God's Commands and respect for those He puts in charge over us. When hatred defines the culture, and is used to bring people to power, Satan is the one who actually wins. The Pilgrims came to America to escape the religious/political hatred (war) in Europe where people where dying on both sides of a war over "I'm saved and you're not". We may be witnessing a regeneration of that same war - in a different time and a different place - with no common ground. Both sides wondering about the future and how they will defend the righteousness of their cause.

The Pilgrims may have been the first to experiment with a new way of communal living evidence by the Mayflower Compact. Their socialist commune lasted a few years but was describe as a dismal failure by William Bradford the governor of Plymouth Plantation. Free enterprise (Capitalism) replace that failed system and the rest is history. If this Great American Experiment fails, there is no place to go to escape. With all the obvious disinformation in the media today, I feel like "Big Brother" is already calling the shots.

"The Red Scare" has become "The Red Wave".

THE SEDUCTION

If I could do one thing to bring about change in the Church today, I would shift the focus of the leadership from sin and salvation (ref. Rom. 6:23) to the purity of lordship. The reason is that without a focus on purity of life and The Lordship of Jesus Christ there is no salvation and no eternal life in the Kingdom. Because of a Reformation, that reformed little or nothing, and a theology that requres nothing but belief, the last 500 to 600 years of Christianity has been chaotic.

There is a good example of this point in 1John 1:9 and how it is translated. First John 1:9 is often used in altar calls to conversion and the awarding of salvation. "If we confess our sins, he is faithful and just and will forgive our sins and purify us from all unrighteousness." NIV. Note that "will forgive our sins" is not in the Greek - instead we should read, "will remove from (His) memory for us our sin natures and sins," "The Pure Word". This verse is about the purification of the mind leading to the purification of the whole person. The (His) I added above only makes sense and makes this passage have more to do with how God sees us and less about how we see ourselves.

Seeking the Kingdom and purity go hand in hand, "But seek first his Kingdom and his righteousness, and all these things shall be given to you as well." Mat. 6:33. The danger in the shifting of focus that we find in 1John 1:9 can not be underestimated. There is the real possibility that the relationship with God will become a chaotic series of "one night stands" - having hedonistic adventures interrupted by spiritual moments of repentance, when needed.

Associating Calvinism with the Reformation is ridiculous. At one extreme French Calvinist celebrated gratuitous sexuality (from the arms of a harlot to the arms of God) to English Puritans who at the extreme found sexuality to be gratuitous even inside of marriage if done only for pleasure. In Calvinism, Jesus is a nice addition to however one wants to live life. "For the time will come when men will not put up with sound doctrine. Instead, to suit their own desires, they will gather around them a great number of teachers to say what their itching ears want to hear." 2Tim 4:3.

The "God forsaken me" last cry of Jesus from the Cross we find in Matthew 27:46 is a stark reminder of those who weep and gnash their teeth at His return. Those who are missguided and ill-prepared for His Second Coming. Peter describes and warns of these same things in his second letter. Second Peter chapters 2&3 may well summarize what I have shared in this book.

The best compliment that I have received on "The death of the Promise" was from a friend who said that I come against Calvinism at every turn. I hope that he was right and I am guilty of that offense. Finding a place of comfort in this chaos seems to be the goal of most Church leaders. That place of comfort is somewhere between - Calvin was wrong (Arminianism) and 5 point hyper Calvinism (Antinomianism).

I find comfort in being a witness to the faith of Abraham and the faith of Paul - waiting on the Child of The Promise and the awarding of my inheritance at His Second Coming. "If you belong to Christ, then you are Abraham's seed and heirs according to The Promise" Gal 3:29. At Jesus' return I will also be a witness to all those who are being condemned.

That troubles me a great deal because I have friends and loved ones who have been seduced by a theology having that wrong focus and faith. What happens when we die is not nearly as important as what happens when Jesus comes back.

The instant gratification appeal found in the Church today was not in the First Century Church. God used the "Soon Coming King" appeal to keep a high level of anticipation of Christ's return - bringing salvation - and giving meaning and purpose to the Church at its birth.

That element had to be there at first but has been lost in the Church today. The hope of Christ's return to fulfill The Promise of Resurrection should and must continue to reside in the Church - keeping the "Blessed Hope" alive. This is the purity of purpose needed in the Church today to foster purity of life in God's people. The logical conclusion follows that man has created a church to serve man's own purpose - a church that tickles itching ears.

Man's impatience continues to lead to the demise of the God of the Old Testament. He has been replaced by an instant gratification God in Jesus who is thought to fight our battles, clean up our messes, give us salvation the moment we believe and take us to Heaven the moment we die. This is in stark contrast to the God I read about in the Old Testament.

In Daniel 9, we find Daniel's prayer of confession. He is 85 years old - has been in captivity for 70 of those years and is confessing the sins of his people - God's people. Immediatly after his prayer we find the 70 weeks of Daniel and God's answer that comes with Christ's death on the Cross - nearly 500 years later. God is not an instant gratification God and neither is Jesus. The Jews had substituted a hope for a warrior king to clean up their mess and fight their battles rather than waiting for the real thing.

God formed Christ's Church around the delayed gratification of salvation at His return, when you lose that - you lose everything.

The unity of faith and hope in Christ's return is the glue that holds the Church together. Instant gratification seems to be the sharpest tool in Satan's tool box. Delayed gratification seems to be the sharpest tool in God's tool box.

> When the instant gratification crowd told God's people that Christ's work on the Cross was a complete work of salvation - poof - no more glue.

Paul opens his first letter to the Corinthians with his concern for division inside the Church. Converts to the faith have put their faith in people rather than like Paul's faith in the promise of Jesus' return. He ends that passage with his concern, and the consequences, for those who are getting their faith wrong - verse 18, "For the message of the cross is foolishness to those who are perishing, but to us who are being saved it is the power of God."

A SUMMARY AND A CONCLUSION

There's a New Sheriff in Town

As the Romans expanded their empire, their means to purify the minds of those they conquered was the threat of the cross. There was a new sheriff in town and obedience to Roman Law was the goal. That cross now represents the Christian Faith and Jesus Christ is now the new sheriff in town. Grace, the freedom from punishment for sin, and The Promise of eternal life is the means by which the mind is purified under the law of love. This is a pure gift to the whole World. Those who understand this pure gift respond by purifying themselves as a conquered people like a bride purifies herself for her wedding day.

The First Century Church lived in anticipation of Christ, the bridegrooms return, and lived in preparation for that event. Faith in Christ's promise to return and fulfill God's promise to Abraham - the resurrection of the dead - was the gift and purity of the Church was to be the response. That hope was to be shared with the whole world as a witness to the faith of Abraham and those first Christians. When Abraham chose to believe God and put his faith in His promise of the resurrection of the dead, he set the pattern of faith for all time. His faith was in The Promise to be fulfilled, not so much in the person (Messiah) that would come to deliver the message. That person, Jesus, has come to deliver the message and will come again to fulfill The Promise. Paul predicts "A Great Falling Away" from this faith. He also predicts – departing from this historic faith will happen before Christ's return.

The problem with focusing on faith in The Church today, it is a word without definition. Hebrews 11:1, "Faith is being sure of what is hoped for, and certain of what is not (yet) seen." The focus of The Book of Hebrews is – the importance of putting our faith in Christ's Second Coming. That faith in The Second Coming defined the faith of those first followers of Jesus. They lived in anticipation and preparation for that moment. That moment was The Day of the Lord, The Day of Salvation and The Day of Redemption. It was the Day that Jesus would come back to award to them what had been promised - "...A Second Time He shall Spiritually Appear to those without sin nature and sin Waiting for Salvation." Hebrews 9:28 - from the Greek- from "The Pure Word". This faith was the glue that would hold The Church together. When His first coming is defined as a complete work of salvation there is no more glue and no more reason to have that faith. However, faith is a word that individuals now define for themselves.

This is the one faith that needs to be taught in all churches. This is right because this is exactly what Paul says in 2Tim. 4:6-8. Paul gives us a sense that, not only is he worthy of his calling, he is also worthy of his reward and then he gives us a really good definition of his faith - The Faith. "For I am already being poured out like a drink offering, and the time has come for my departure. I have fought the good fight, I have finished the race, I have kept the faith. Now there is in store for me a crown of righteousness, which the Lord, the righteous Judge, will award to me on that day (Day) - Not only to me, but also to all who (like me) have longed for his appearing."

Unsaid in this passage, but apparent, is the joy of looking back on his adventure. From before his conversion to longing to see Jesus at the end of the line, he is satisfied with his journey of Kingdom service. It is a combination of the joy of the journey and the joy of the destination. It is a joy and adventure Paul might have missed if the Spirit of Jesus had told him he was eternally secure at his conversion - and, more importantly, he would have had no basis for making this statement at the end of his life.

Again, this is The Faith that needs to be taught in our churches as Paul instructs us to teach the unity of The Faith in Eph. 4:1, 11-13. (...so that the body of Christ may be built up until we all reach unity in the faith and in the knowledge of the Son of God...)

This is a most important part of the Gospel Paul preached. This is The Faith that is in my heart that I will take to Judgment - It is The Faith in Jesus' Second Coming and the reason why - it was The Faith of The First Century Church. It is a faith - and a hope - and a promise - that all who will go into the Kingdom will hold in common.

As Pharisees, both Paul and Nicodemus were taught from birth the full knowledge of their salvation. In John 3, Jesus tells Nicodemus he must be born again to a new vision without which he cannot see the Kingdom. Peter, in his first letter, begins in verse 3 by praising God for being born anew into a living hope (living in hope) of salvation. Faith in this living hope results in "for you are receiving the goal of your faith, the salvation of your souls." verse 9. "Earning the End of Faith for yourselves, the Salvation of you souls." The Pure Word. Earned salvation? Yes, through a pure and genuine faith. What a difference a word makes - receiving vs earning.

John 3:16 in the Greek actually connects lordship (commitment) to eternal life, not belief. This passage from John 2:23 to John 3:21 is more about exclusion and less about inclusion and those whose commitment is not sufficient to the need to enter the Kingdom. When Jesus looks into the believer's heart, those without commitment are judged and condemned this side of the grave. Lordship (commitment) and a genuine faith are the keys to the Kingdom and salvation. The word commitment in the Greek has the element of putting your entire being under the orders of another. Verses 19-21 make clear that committing to the truth brings one into the light and is pivotal in Final Judgment. The verdict is based on true and genuine commitment in both judgments mentioned here.

There is an irony that comes out of John 3 in that those who have unbelief, or wrong belief, are judged and condemned this side of the grave. The idea that belief is the evidence of salvation is wrong - commitment is the evidence of salvation and will be judged when Jesus comes back. Those who believe that at the moment you die, you go to heaven are wrong. What do they do with Final Judgment and that verdict? They put themselves in the place of Judgment before they die and are condemned this side of the grave for their wrong belief. Don't say you love Jesus if you don't love the truth.

EPILOGUE

The Appearance of Impropriety

In this book I have touched on the crisis on the southern border which has gotten dramatically worse. It is obvious that opening the border is designed to move the American electorate in favor of the Democrats. I hope those immigrants, and others, realize they are about to vote for politicians whose ambition is to have a government just like the governments they are trying to escape. In the past those who were taken advantage of like this, were described as "useful idiots" and then starved to death as they competed for a diminished food supply. If this situation is coming, it will not be local, it will be world wide. This is a man-made crisis of epic proportions.

Another crisis of epic proportions is the Covid-19 crisis. More and more evidence is coming out that this too, is a man-made crisis that came out of a laboratory in China. It was knowingly exported to world through international air travel. If you look at those who cried the loudest when President Trump shut down air travel to China, you will very likely find those in America who supported this plot. This crisis played a major roll in defeating President Trump in his re-election bid. It is now time to make the connection between political ambition in the Democrat Party and China - connecting the dots and the appearence of Impropriety. In a campaign Appearance Barack Obama denegrated deficit government spending as, "spending money on a credit card from the Bank of China on our children's or maybe our grandchildren's lives", a thought stolen from the Republicans. This was diabolical - by making people believe that his political opponent was going to do exactly what he was planning to do. In eight years, Obama's government doubled America's national debt. In the same way he reveals his, and the Democrat party's, China Connection. I see people like this as very evil.

In an appearance before his inauguration Obama said this "We are five days away from the fundamental transformation of America." We are now seeing this in real time at home but especially in Afganistan and also seeing the China Connection. The end game to date in Afganistan is human misery and drama covering up the transfer of Bagram Air Force Base from The American Military to the Chinese Military - along with as much as $100,000,000,000 (billions) in state of the art military weaponry. This was done quietly and in such a way that hardly anyone noticed - just turn out the lights, put the key in the door and leave. Much to the joy of Chairman Chi - giving aid and comfort to a global enemy and with a giant, well placed, state of the art air force base to boot. China's Military moving in as quietly as The America Military left.

As America re-built Bagram AFB it became a gun pointed at the head of Chairman Chi. It is obvious that Chairman Chi, at some point in time, told the Obama White House that he wanted that threat to go away. The hatred that was generated by the Democrat Party against President Trump was the means by which he could be defeated and thus Chairman Chi would aquire Bagram, turn the gun around and point it at the head of anyone else (a head of state) who got in his way. Boldly making the World unsafe for democracies and freedom loving peope where ever they may be found.

Recently, our Secretary of State testified that the Biden White House inherited a deadline and no plan. Just the opposite was true. President Trump's plan was to keep that gun pointed at Chairman Chi's head and at the same time pointed at the heads of Talaban leaders (air support for the Afgan Army). There was no plan to withdraw from Bagram at any time. Defeating President Trump by hook by crook was at the pleasure of Chairman Chi. The Biden White House wasted no time in moving ahead with their plan to turn over Bagram to China. For Joe Biden and the Democrats, political ambition has alway been the name of the game and the collateral damage and loss of life that resulted from this plan was, and is, acceptable to them. When one looks at Obama's history of associating with the likes of Sol Alinski, Bill Ayers, Jerimiah Wright, Van Jones and other radical/revolutionaries - it is easy to see where this plan was hatched.

Deserting Bagram was never a part of President Trump's plan. While the Democrats were crying Russian collusion, the China Connection with the Democrats was trying in every way possible to get him out of office. President Trump had interrupted a planned 16 year campaign to fundamentally transform America, you see Clinton and Obama are cut from the same cloth and with the same goals. You can be sure, with his office in DC, Obama would have been calling the shots in a Clinton White House just like he is doing today in the Biden White House.

The China Connection with the Democrats is obvious, they both want to fundanamentally transform America and achieving a "One World Order" is their goal. This is a spiritual war because there is no place for any religion in a "One World Order" world.

I touch on a lot of this in the book and what happened with Bagram brought it all into focus. I didn't miss this because my business partner and our company did a lot of work at Bagram. I don't believe they could get by with this if they didn't own the propaganda wing of the China Connection - The Main Stream Media.

There is an axiom that is used by people who are bent on evil; "The enemy of my enemy is my friend". It comes from Islam. There is no mystery as to how the suicide bomber got so close to our American troops. There is no mystery on how China got Bagram - Chairman Chi and the Democrat Party and their supporters have a common enemy - they hate President Trump and all those who support him. I would suggest that what is going on today in our government, with China and the Democrats being on the same page, is just that - The Biden White House is a puppet of Red China. What is on Hunter Biden's lap-top will go a long way to prove this to be true. China getting Bagram was a giant leap forward toward a godless "One World Order". The balance of power in the world has shifted and China may have already won the battle of Armageddon without firing a shot.

As I look back on all that I have been led to write, God seems to be unlocking a mystery surrounding the murder of 13 of our service men among many others killed and wounded (collateral damage). The appearance of impropriety of Hunter Bidien receiving millions of unearned dollars and President Trump asking the President of Ukrane to investigate this was stopped dead in its tracks. This investigation may have unlocked the mystery of Hunter accompanying his dad on a trip to China and revealed the China Connection and just maybe a $1.5 billion down payment on Bagram AFB. The fear of such an investigation unhinged the leadership of the Democrat Party - it had to be stopped. An Impeachment, which had no basis in fact was their solution - killing two birds with one stone. Hunter's lap-top will in all probability unlock this mystery and point to those ultimately responsible for those murders.

When Joe Biden drew a comparison of his son Beau's death from brain cancer to the deaths of those 13 service men, he drew a perfect picture of his methods, their madness and shared dream of transformation. Biden, Obama and all those who share this dream of a transformed America are a cancer on The American Dream. Those 13 service men were there to preserve, protect and defend our American Dream - from all enemies, both foreign and domestic of our Constitution. They were there for all those who love this land as it is - and wish to pass that Dream on to the next generation.

"Anyone who hates his brother is a murderer, and you know that no murderer has eternal life in him." 1John 3:15

"Wolves in sheep's clothing...You will know them by their fruit." Jesus, from the Sermon on the Mount.

THE LAND OF THE PROMISE
BOOK 3 OF THE TRILOGY

PICKING UP
WHERE I LEFT OFF

It has become obvious to me that God is leading me to complete a trilogy that I have titled "on that Day". "The Land of the Promise" is the title of this third and final book of the trilogy focused on the fulfillment of The Promise God made to Abraham. The Faith of those first followers of Jesus was very much tied to His return and "on that Day" the awarding of salvation. I have characterized those First-Century Christians, who are waiting and watching for this event, as attending a "Watch Party". This is a faith in that coming event as much as it is faith in the person who made The Promise to return.

In the back of my first book "The Road to Restoration", I say that the Christian Culture has been hi-jacked by the instant gratification crowd which became a recurring theme of the first two books of this trilogy. So, with that in mind, let me pick up where I left off in book 2, "The Resurrection of The Promise". What this may be is an abbreviated summary of what I have already written, with the addition of identifying the grave consequence of being a part of the instant gratification crowd.

A dear friend who helped me a great deal in my writing with constructive criticism - loved the book up to the last chapter. I wrote that chapter when censoring of the internet had become a hot topic. My publisher suggested to me the I write a book about my feelings in that area. I decided that I could do it in a chapter and so I did thinking that they would edit it out of the book. When that didn't happen, I had a crisis of belief. Was God prompting me or not? While deep down, I really liked how it came together. I had written what I felt needed to be said and would never get another chance to say it to the whole world. Don't throw the baby out with the bath water.

THE FULFILLMENT
OF THE PROMISE

The plot to kill Jesus first appears in Chapter 5 of John's Gospel and it became a political plot in order to get it done. Barabbas, there can be no doubt, was a political prisoner. His name was actually Jesus - notoriously known as Barabbas (son of the father - the High Priest). He was surely in the family of the High Priest and had been raised in hope that he would become the warrior king (Messiah) that the Jews wanted in order to rid themselves of the Romans. I think it is important to understand how politics and religion can be made to work together to further an agenda - good or bad.

Barabbas was not just a common criminal; he was a radical revolutionary who had political value - an insurrectionist. A person caught robbing was not put in jail - he was immediately crucified. Jesus was also a radical revolutionary at a moment in time where the Jews, as a matter of convenience, could trade an innocent man for a guilty man. Only God could orchestrate a situation such as this, as prophesied by Daniel, at that exact moment in time. It must be noted here that the Koran portrays an innocent man, who looked like Jesus, having been substituted for Jesus and crucified. Jesus was crucified in order to save Barabbas' life. In any event,

Jesus was collateral damage to a political agenda and just maybe the Jews were killing two birds with one stone. The more things change - the more they stay the same.

Paul would qualify as a radical revolutionary who was eventually killed for that offense. Our founding fathers would also qualify, as would John Wesley, a hero of the faith. Wesley was a radical revolutionary against the Church of England and was very careful to stay within the law or else he very likely would have been executed. The freedom to be a radical revolutionary is quickly disappearing unless it is for the cause of "One World Order".

I am at war with the instant gratification culture and the leadership that promotes that agenda in The Church. There is a parable in Scripture that very pointedly addresses those who want instant citizenship in the Kingdom and do not want to wait on Jesus, the Righteous Judge, to go away and then to return bringing His Kingdom with him, (Reference - The Lord's Prayer). It is the Parable of The Minas starting at Luke 19:11. This passage was brought to my attention recently and caused me to get serious about adding to what I had already written.

I recommend to you read this for yourself in whatever Bible version you use, and zero in on verse 11 - "instantly" in the Greek, then verse 14 and 27 - lordship and citizenship denied. The phrase "weeping and gnashing of teeth", that we find in some passages of Judgment, could be coming from Jesus as He is not willing that anyone should perish.

This is a watch party of a different sort. After the king returns, he and his subjects watch as those who are condemned are executed in front of them just as Jesus instructs them to do. In Matthew 25 we find a similar story (The Parable of the Talents) with the weeping and gnashing of teeth at that Judgment - not a pretty sight. Next door, and prior to this, we find the Parable of the Ten Virgins where a watch party turned into a slumber party waiting on the bridegroom to return. We witness the joy of the wise virgins and the sorrow of the foolish virgins and then the instruction to be prepared and keep watch.

There is a contrast here between the two groups. The wise virgins display The Faith of The First-Century Church living in expectation and preparation for the soon coming bridegroom. The foolish virgins display the faith of the lukewarm - Laodicean Church. Lamps without oil, faith without focus, purpose or definition - The Twenty-First-Century Church displaying The Great Falling Away from The Faith prophesied by Paul.

THE UNITY OF THE FAITH

In the Parable of The Minas we find perhaps the most important Instruction on faith in the Bible without mentioning the word. These evil men do not want to be ruled by a king that comes back as The Righteous Judge. They are critical of his judgment here, and most of all, they would or could never have The Faith of The First-Century Church. In Ephesians 4, Paul writes that all efforts in the Body of Christ are to be reaching for Unity of The Faith. That one faith is in Jesus's promise to return as The Righteous Judge bringing salvation with Him. God's plan of salvation works only with The Second Coming as the end game of man being restored to Paradise.

I can't decide on who says this best, Paul or Peter, so let us listen to both. Paul, in 2 Timothy 4:7-8, says,"...I have kept the faith. Now there is in store for me a crown of righteousness which the Lord, the righteous judge, will award to me on that day - not only to me, but also to all who have (loved and) longed for his appearing." Peter, in 1 Peter 1:3-5, says, "Praise be to the God and Father of our Lord Jesus Christ! In his great mercy he has given us new birth into a living hope through the resurrection of Jesus Christ from the dead, and into an inheritance that can never perish, spoil or fade - kept in heaven for you, who through faith are shielded by God's power until the coming of salvation that is ready to be revealed at the last time (Day)."

Jesus's work on the Cross is portrayed in today's culture as a complete work of salvation and the end game in God's plan of salvation. In this culture, all efforts are directed at saving souls. Jesus Himself says this in Luke 19:10, "For the son of man came to seek and to save what was lost." The focus on salvation, versus the focus on Unity of The Faith, is a life-or-death situation. What follows Luke 19:10 is The Parable of the Minas and the consequence for those who want the story to end without The Second Coming and the coming of The Righteous Judge. Little if any faith is required for salvation - only belief. Faith in The Second Coming is critical in God's plan of salvation because "without faith, it is impossible to please God." This is The Faith of The First-Century Church.

Jesus does a really good job of bringing all of this together in Luke 9:21 and following, "...The son of man must suffer many things and be rejected by the elders and high priests and teachers of the law, and he must be killed and on the third day be raised to life. Then he said to them all, 'If anyone would come after me, he must deny himself and take up his cross daily and follow me.... whoever loses his life for me will save it.' "

Notice that the moment of decision is followed by a very demanding faith journey of unconditional surrender. Jesus does not mention the nature and manner of His death but does show the nature and manner of a life lived in anticipation of salvation and life eternal - a consequence for both Him and those that choose to follow Him in this manner. The demands that Jesus puts on His followers here are much the same as the demands He puts on Himself.

Notice also that a phrase has been purposefully omitted in the quote above from Luke 9. "For whoever wants to save his life will lose it, but...". Focusing on what's at the end of the journey is a sin unto death, so focusing on the journey itself is the life that leads to life eternal. Could it be any plainer and easier to understand? Today's culture has put salvation at the beginning of the journey and thus omits the need for the faith journey that Jesus describes here - creating the lukewarm church of today.

Close to the end of John's first letter he mentions, "There is a sin that leads to death". This is put on display vividly in The Parable of the Minas. Jesus portrays this instant gratification crowd as hating a king that would make a second coming and righteous judgment the end game of their salvation. It is hard for anyone in the Church to see themselves as hating our King, but it must be the way Jesus sees the instant gratification crowd and thus their death sentence. Having the mind of Christ, we must see this through His eyes and follow His demands. There is no need to focus on salvation, salvation will take care of itself for those who have made Jesus Lord of their life and have The Faith of The First- Century Church.

THE MIND OF CHRIST

How to rewire the saved mind-set is the question that must be answered. It may be creating a "foxhole" mentality in our leaders. "Lord if I get out of this situation, I'll teach and preach the Unity of The Faith the rest of my life". The instant gratification crowd is headed to a spiritual firing squad if they don't repent. If what happens at The Second Coming is not pivotal in your understanding of God's plan of salvation, you have a counterfeit faith and are, therefore, a counterfeit christian. The words of the hymn "The Solid Rock" come to mind, "When He shall come with trumpet sound - oh may I then in Him be found - dressed in His righteousness alone - faultless before the throne". In Jude vs 24,"...to present you before his glorious presence without fault and with great joy.".

The whole of The New Testament seems to say that eternal life begins with the decision of belief and commitment. This must be followed by an earthly faith journey with an accounting at Jesus's return - at the resurrection of the dead. It must be an accounting of what was done and why it was done. From the beginning of time, The Promise of eternal life has been with us, but is not fulfilled until Jesus comes back for this final accounting. This Final Judgment is ignored in most, if not all, invitations to be saved. Final Judgment becomes a non-issue for the whole culture because of this omission. This results in a counterfeit gospel, a counterfeit faith, a counterfeit truth and of course a counterfeit church. In 2 Timothy 3, Paul is very descriptive of this reality - in the last days - and a gospel that has no power to save.

Verse 5, "having the form of godliness but denying its power."

Verse7, "always learning but never able to acknowledge the truth."

Verse 8, "...these men oppose the truth - men of depraved minds who are, as far as the faith is concerned, are rejected." (grace denied)

The tension in the stories in Matthew chapters 24&25 is not between believers and non-believers, it is between those who have a genuine faith and those who have a counterfeit faith. These people need to have their minds rewired and, in a sense, have the stone rolled away from in front of their eyes. Putting the truth in front of believers is the first step in pushing against the darkness, but only God can roll the stone away.

The foundation of what is being taught in our churches today is the total depravity of man. The way to escape that prison is to believe that at the moment of belief escape is possible only by buying into this dogma. This parallels the "Critical Race Theory" of today, which is based on the total depravity of the white man. The only way to escape that prison is to buy into that dogma and receive a "get-out-of-jail-free" card at the moment of belief. One destroys the relationship between God and man - the other destroys human relationships. Both have the effect of promoting "One World Order"- destroying The Church for a political agenda.

Destroying relationships between generations, destroying relationships within families, destroying relationships between the races, destroying relationships between political parties - the list goes on. The hatred that has developed in America between people is both obvious and tragic. Jesus lays this developing hatred at the feet of the instant gratification crowd in the Parable of the Minas - Verse 14, "But his subjects hated him and sent a delegation after him to say, 'We don't want this man to be our king". These men hated the delayed gratification of The Second Coming and the Righteous Judge. They had to develop a counterfeit god - an instant gratification god - an idol and substitute for the real thing.

Just like Moses taking a long time coming down from the mountain and The Golden Calf - The Parable of the Minas depicts a similar situation. When Moses sees The Golden Calf, God tells him He wants to kill them all because his anger burned against them. Moses appealed to God not to kill them all - these were His chosen people. Both stories depict rebellion against God. The definition of sin is rebellion against God and is in The Church today for all those who have ignored Final Judgment and this future accounting. Moral impurity had taken over the Hebrew's camp and God's judgment was very, very far from their minds.

MERGING HEAVEN AND EARTH

The Blessed Hope we find in the book of Titus is not the hope of Heaven, it is the hope of Jesus's return and Him finding a spotless unblemished bride, His Church, watching and waiting for Him. He comes back to dwell with His people on this Earth. There will be no need to keep Heaven and Earth separated anymore. So Paradise is the restoration of the Garden of Eden where God and man dwelled together as it was in the beginning on this Earth.

In a sense the fire associated with this restoration seems to be a metaphor for the purification of God's own righteous anger and mankind's rebellion and resistance to God's plan of salvation. Thus giving a new start to the God - man relationship in a paradise without sin and sin nature. Just as if sin and God's righteous anger never happened. John, in 1 John 1:9, captures this mind-set as he writes, "If we should continuously Confess our sin natures and sins, He is Faithful and Righteous to Remove from Memory for us the sin natures and sins, that He might Cleanse us from all unrighteousness." (The Pure Word)

This makes so much sense to me now and God leading me to write out this trilogy helped me to make sense of what made no sense to me before. A psychologist once gave me some tests that resulted in finding that I processed information very differently from most people. There are many people who let me know that the instant gratification culture that has grown up in America is ruining our Country and our Church. Pushing against that darkness is Jesus's story - make it your story.

The phrase, "God's Plan of Salvation", is very important to understand. Nothing happens in this world without God's foreknowledge. Writing this plan out and putting it on paper and making sense of it all is just as important. God is coming back to a world from which He removed Himself. After the fall, His presence in this world is through His Spirit - His prophets and He occasionally steps out of Heaven to speak to His People directly. Abraham's encounter with God was an important encounter between God and man. God's direction and Abraham's unconditional surrender, secured The Promise for Abraham's descendants and, by extension, for you and me.

Living in The Promise of resurrection had died in The Jewish Culture so God in Jesus set foot on the Earth once more to preach, teach and resurrect The Promise. The Age of Grace - Sanctifying Grace and growing in the knowledge of God, between Jesus's First and Second Coming, is the final stage of God's plan of salvation. Jesus and the Father come back and set foot again on the Earth to unite Heaven and Earth and dwell with God's people for eternity.

In The Parable of The Minas we find no forgiveness and no second chance. Those who have done well - pleasing the king - earned their reward. Those did poorly - displeasing the king - were punished severely. The Faith of The First-Century Church is critical to The Righteous Judge and to His Chosen People. The emotions we see in Jesus in this passage reach a critical point when He enters the temple and His anger explodes as He drives out the money changers. Then we find the Parable of The Tenants and more murder and mayhem. This is the last of the story of His first coming and His murder, but it is not the end of the story. Before

Stephen is martyred in Acts 7, he says this in verse 52, " Was there ever a prophet your fathers did not persecute? They even killed those who predicted the coming of the Righteous One. And now you have betrayed and murdered him."

There can be no doubt that Paul was there and heard this. He shortly encountered the Spirit of Jesus on the road to Damascus. His conversion is important to understand. As a Pharisee, Paul believed that he already possessed eternal life and the moment he died, he would be resurrected into the age to come - paradise or heaven.

His conversion was dramatic and a complete - turning away from that belief. Though his conversion was dramatic and instantaneous, it took him years to share his new faith with the world. His faith was no longer in the possession of eternal life and instantly going to heaven - his faith was in a journey that defined his new faith and The Blessed Hope of the award of eternal life at Jesus's return. Relating this reality and linking it to these last two parables in Luke seems so important that it bears repeating. Nothing is more important in the salvation story than what happens at Jesus's Second Coming. Anyone who thinks they get into the Kingdom any other way will find out at Judgment - grace denied.

GRACE REJECTED

A very subtle element in The Parable of The Minas is the rejection of living in The Promise of salvation. You can't recognize this if you don't understand that The Promise God made to Abraham is yet to be fulfilled. We can also see Satan at work in the hearts of these people who hate the king and are on a mission to defeat this plan. Grace denied is the consequence of grace rejected. When I go back and read the blurb on the back of my first book "The Road To Restoration", it gives me time to pause and think how God led me to pursue the truth of The Parable of the Minas - without knowing it was in the Bible. This is what I wrote six years ago:

> "While I have worked on this project for two years, about half way through, I told my pastor that I felt like I was taking on the whole John 3:16 Christian culture. While I have never believed that at the moment of belief or surrender, we receive the keys to the kingdom, I have come to the understanding that Jesus is telling Nicodemus who He is and what He is going to do at His second coming. He takes care of the sin problem and shows that He has the power over death at His first coming, initiates the age of true righteousness and sets the stage

for His second coming. It is at this time that he lifts the curse and completes the promise made to Abraham, reveals who the children of God are and establishes His kingdom here on this earth. <u>On that Day,</u> the dead in Christ will come out of the grave and meet Him in the air.

We have a choice of whether to believe that Jesus completes the work of salvation at His first coming or His second coming. There are so many scriptures that place the complete work of salvation at His second coming, that I find it difficult to believe that He completes this work at His first coming. It comes down to mankind's desire for instant gratification.

In Luke 9, there is a passage where Jesus, before He picks up His cross, once and for all time, talks specifically about who He is and what He has come to do at His first coming. In this passage, He tells His disciples that they, too, along with all those who choose to follow Him, must pick up their cross daily. This does not appeal to the instant gratification crowd, but it is where faith begins. Where our faith journey begins determines where our journey will end."

I believe my writing has improved a great deal, but the message has not changed. The underlining above of "on that Day" is added to make this point. The Parable of the Minas proves The Faith of The First-Century Church is absolute. It is the faith that saves. What began as an adventure in discovery in Scripture, along with being counter-cultural, has led me to very uncomfortable place.

Turning evidence into proof is a scary thing when it involves the whole culture. Just like in the last election, very few people in powerful positions wanted to look at the evidence of a stolen election and take a chance that it might prove to be true.

Stringing Scriptures together is a technique used by many to create a gospel of their own making. When the Parables of The Ten Virgins and The Minas are brought together, they draw a clear picture of The Faith that saves. Paul makes this clear in 2Timothy 4:6-8. In spite of this, the instant gratification crowd seem to be intent on leading the Christian Culture to the slaughter described in The Minas. In their haste, they have strung together Scriptures and left out the return of The Righteous Judge, the accounting of what has been done and the awarding of that crown of righteousness at The Second Coming. "I delight greatly in the Lord; my soul rejoices in my God. For he has clothed me in garments of salvation and arrayed me in a robe of righteousness, as a bridegroom adorns his head like a priest, and as a bride adorns herself with her jewels." (Isaiah 61:10).

It's about time the truth comes out that the focus on salvation is a marketing scheme that has been refined over the centuries to suit man's agenda which is clearly a sin unto death, "For whoever wants to save his life will lose it, but whoever loses his life for me will save it." (Luke 9:23). The joy of meeting Jesus in the air, face-to-face, standing on this earth will be short-lived. Those few who got their faith right will be a witness to the consequences of the many who got their faith wrong. It will be a watch party of a different sort and a sorrowful event for all those who are there - and particularly for Jesus.

Luke 9:23 is a message for those leaders who have bought into this marketing scheme. If, and when, they repent of this sin unto death, they will have to face dying for the truth. There will be "hell to pay" for The Culture when the truth comes out that salvation is not something to be marketed (tickling itching ears). Jesus comes out of Heaven to push against the darkness. A culture vested in a lie is doomed and, until the leadership repents, there is no hope for salvation for the entire culture. Those who understand this must take the lead and then lead (I am) "The Way To The Truth and To The Life".

It is interesting that to do a good job in translating Greek one must add prepositional phrases at times to make it clear what is being said. For example, in that last paragraph, in the last sentence, the prepositions bring more understanding to what Jesus is saying. And like the exchange between Jesus and The Thief on the Cross, where to place the comma is not the real problem. By substituting a prepositional phrase for ",Today", one can get a better understanding of the exchange. "Jesus, remember me when you come into your kingdom." Jesus answered him, "I tell you the truth, on that Day you will be with me in paradise." (Luke 23:42-43)

Paul uses that same phrase, "on that Day" in 2Timothy 4:8 referring to his meeting with Jesus at His return. Our destiny is not in a place, it is a predetermined meeting with The Righteous Judge at His return. It is at this meeting that our destiny is determined. From the beginning of time, God knows what the outcome of this meeting will be and awards His children according to what they have done.

It must be noted that I don't know how the word predestination found its way into the New Testament, but it was identified by John Wesley as foundationally leading to lawlessness and the moral decay of the Church Culture.

This is an example of how important what happens at Jesus's return is and how unimportant it is in our culture. Pushing against this darkness is like pulling teeth. Jesus makes this accounting a part of His Sermon on the Mount in Matthew 6:1-18 which includes The Lord's Prayer. He contrasts rewards fulfilled in the past with rewards that are fulfilled in the future. These are instructions for those who are on the journey, doing things in a way that displeases or pleases God.

This fits in with The Promise of the return of The Righteous Judge and an accounting of what has been done and why it was done. There is no instant gratification here, only doing the right thing, for the right reason, and with a future reward. Jesus puts His prayer right in the middle of this passage with a warning. Not doing so will have grave consequences - losing His forgiveness means losing The Promise. In so many passages like this one, Jesus gives us good instructions on someone to love, something to do and something to look forward to. "If you love me, you will obey what I command." John 14:15

This shows the character of God and the righteousness of those who choose to follow Jesus. Pleasing God in our "righteous acts" is no less important than a genuine faith that pleases Him also. "And without faith it is impossible to please God...", Hebrews 11:6. This is why it is critically important to know The Faith of The First Century Church and why it is critically important for us to take that same genuine faith to The Final Judgment. Grace denied is the consequence of grace rejected (refused). Righteous acts plus a genuine faith enables a Just God to reward and fulfill The Promise He made to Abraham.

Putting The Parable of The Minas together with The Parable of The Ten Virgins has opened my eyes to a whole new understanding of why I get such a cool reception from people when I talk about The Faith of The First Century Church. The lukewarm church doesn't want to hear the wisdom of The First Century Church because it reveals their foolishness. Rev. 3:20 has been so misused as to create the lukewarm church instead of warning against it and avoiding it.

"Behold, I stand at the door and knock...", is not Jesus knocking on the door of our heart. It is The Holy Spirit knocking on the door of the lukewarm church of today wanting to be heard and have the door opened to Him. With this change in the dynamic, the idea that we have welcomed Jesus into our heart takes hold and it follows that Jesus must welcome us into His Heaven. In typical liberal fashion, preachers create the problem and then come riding in to save the day. Like serial arsonists, they firebomb the Church and then show up to put out the fire. They preach against the lukewarm church and try to convince us to catch fire for the Gospel. For those who think they are already saved, it lands on deaf ears. Why do anything if I'm already saved? And of course, anything a preacher can talk us into in thirty minutes - Satan can talk us out of in thirty seconds.

In this book, especially these last paragraphs it is obvious that I am trying to undo what the instant gratification crowd has been doing for centuries - focus The Culture on salvation and putting it in the past. From Genessis to Revelation the focus of God's word is on The Day of the Lord. This is the Day that Heaven and Earth are merged (Paradise) and Father, Son and Holy Spirit are merged into the Righteous Judge. The Righteous Judge brings justice and reward and with that populates the Kingdom. Jesus comes the first time to do the groundwork - prepare the seed bed for us to put our hand to the plow - to be productive for the Kingdom and not look back. Keeping our eyes on what's ahead of us, not on what's behind us. On that Day we will be held accountable for what we did with what we were given.

Post Modern Christianity is a do-nothing gospel - we did nothing to earn salvation and need do nothing to keep it. We can live our lives the way we choose without concern for consequences - doing whatever satisfies our physical and emotional needs. The evil doers, lawless believers, we find toward the end of The Sermon on the Mount are the consequence of this modern gospel. These people are those who call Jesus Lord but do not know Him as The Righteous Judge. On that Day they will receive what they have earned and continue in the darkness that they new in this world having rebelled against The Second Coming and the justice that Jesus will bring with Him.

In Luke 6:46-49, we find the Reader's Digest version of The Wise and Foolish Builders, which serves to identify who these lawless believers (evil doers) are. In Luke, the wise man digs down deep to find solid rock on which to build his faith. The foolish man is unconcerned about the foundation and the ground on which his faith rests. Paul leaves no doubt about the foundation of his faith, no wiggle room, when he says, "a faith and knowledge resting on the hope of eternal life...", Titus 3:2 NIV prior to 1968. The Post-Modern Gospel and its predecessor Calvinism requires no such deep-seated faith and hope in The Second Coming.

The thought that at the resurrection we just pick-up where we left off when we die is hard to wrap our mind around. But that must be how it is going to be. Paradise without sin and sin nature - a new beginning - sitting at the banquet table on The Day of the Lord. A celebration to end all celebrations for all who saw the awarding of eternal life as a bonus for a life lived in obedience to the Law Of Love.

"ON THAT DAY"

The use of the word ",Today" is found in Hebrews 3&4 - three of the instances repeating the same quote from Psalms 95. None of these are accurately translated in "Strong's Concordance". Including the exchange with the thief we find ", to day" in Strong's in each instance. In each case it should read, ",on that Day", a reference to The Second Coming". If this is confusing you, you are right. But one thing comes across clearly - this confusion started a long time ago. Psalms 95 verse 1, "O Come, Let us sing for joy to the Lord, let us shout aloud to the Rock of our salvation." is "on that Day" at The Second Coming. And then in verse 7-8, "...Today (on that Day) if you will hear his voice, do not harden your hearts as you did at Meribah" (the rebellion).

This is a fatal flaw in all Bible translations. It leads the Christian Culture to a belief that salvation is instantaneous like The Thief on the Cross. Exactly what Jesus is identifying in the Parable of the Minas in Luke 19:11, "...the people thought that the kingdom of God was going to appear at once." These people are the ",Today" crowd, not wanting to wait for The Second Coming. God has led me, step-by-step, to this conclusion. It is there for anyone to see and to be disturbed as I have been. Paul gathers around him the "on that Day" crowd (including the thief), when he says, "on that Day, and not only me but also to all who have longed for His appearing."

Bible translators, theologians and preachers have all put the Christian Culture in the ",Today" crowd and doomed them to the fate of those who rebel against salvation at The Second Coming. This is especially true at funerals when ministers place the deceased in Heaven. In the first few verses of Romans 10, Paul is very clear in telling us not to place people in Heaven or Hell. When they do that, they are placing themselves, and the deceased, in the ", Today" crowd and into the rebellion.

The real meaning of what Jesus says to the Thief may actually be lost. In order to make it agree with the rest of Scripture, I have inserted what makes sense to me to reduce the confusion. And to include the Thief in the "on that Day" crowd. Jesus does not ascend into Heaven for many days after His death and resurrection. For Him to say to the Thief ",Today you will be with me in paradise" would be dishonest. Jesus meets him again at the resurrection and then welcomes him into Paradise "on that Day".

Paul puts all those who want to be remembered "on that Day" into a "Tomorrow" crowd, focused on the Day Jesus comes back which makes the Christian Faith unique in all world religions. The idea that all of God's children are called out of the grave for a Day of Final Judgment is unique. The idea of that great getting-up morning has disappeared in the Christian Culture. The Faith of The First-Century Church is what makes a person uniquely Christian.

What saved those five wise virgins in their story? When did it happen? The answer is: they were justified (purified) by their faith in The Promise as they resisted the perilous lukewarm church along their journey. They overcame the temptation to become part of the lukewarm church and thus, counterfeit Christians. The Teachers of the Law and Pharisees thought they were saved and resisted living in The Promise of salvation. They were locked out of the kingdom just like those five foolish virgins, and in the same way, believers will be locked out of the Kingdom for the very same foolishness.

The watch party that the five wise virgins enjoyed leads directly to the wedding banquet God has prepared for those who have been faithful to The Promise. To read more about this wedding banquet and counterfeit faith, go to Matthew 22 and see how that parable ends. How the one who did not wear his wedding clothes was treated and the moral of the story, "For many are invited, but few are chosen."

In 2 Timothy 4:6-8, Paul portrays himself as being on deaths doorstep. He then gives us the evidence of his service and then defines his faith - this is the Good News. He puts himself in a place of trusting, watching and waiting. He is the genuine article. Then he gathers together all those who are genuine articles of The Faith into a watch party for those who love, long for and trust in Jesus's return. Genuine Faith in Jesus's return is manifested, compared to the counterfeit faith of the lukewarm Laodicean Church. Two different gospels are spread, one leads to eternal condemnation - the other to eternal life. This is the Gospel according to Paul.

Choosing to believe that you do not receive your reward until Jesus comes back in final judgment makes one a genuine Christian; those who believe they are saved prior to that moment, have chosen to be a counterfeit christian. It is just that simple and yet a serious dilemma for the Christian Culture today. In other words; instant gratification Christianity is counterfeit. The moment of belief and the moment of death are just two of many milestones on "The Road to Restoration", to Judgment and to the awarding of salvation, that "Crown of Righteousness", on that Day.

This faith must be The Faith that saves. It was preordained by Jesus before His departure and gives a very special definition of the word faith in the Christian Community. This is true and must be taught, as such, in our churches so that living in preparation for and anticipation of The Second Coming will dominate the Church Culture. Those first Christians were not saved by grace alone; in addition, they were justified by faith as a response to The Promise of salvation. God's grace is in The Promise which is in the pure gift that Jesus gave them: Someone to love; Something to do; and Something to look forward to.

It is so important to understand that through this aspect of faith, Paul makes this statement in Ephesians 2:8, "For by grace are ye saved through faith, not of yourselves, it is a gift from God", KJV. This special gift gives His followers something to look forward to and levels the playing field so that no one can boast that their faith is stronger than another's. Jesus defines this faith by telling them that He is going away and then will return bringing salvation with Him. "So Christ was once made Offered to Bear Up as in an Offering for the sin natures and sin of many. A second time He Shall Spiritually Appear to those without sin nature and sin Waiting on Salvation.", (Hebrews 9:28) The Pure Word. Notice here that those waiting on salvation have been purified from their sin and sin nature.

The KJV is the only other translation that I have found that has similar wording. "...without sin unto salvation", most other versions have, "waiting for Him." Purification comes from looking forward to The Promise to be fulfilled. Whether from God or our own efforts, looking forward to The Promise to be fulfilled is the key to holiness and purity of The Faith and the key to the Kingdom.

When Jesus calls Lazarus out of the grave in John chapter 11, that was not the end of the day. This was a very emotional day for Jesus and all those present. John details the reaction of the Chief Priests and Pharisees but does not record the reaction of family and friends. There must have been a great celebration that afternoon for sure, but not a word of it in Scripture. Leading up to this event Jesus says to Martha, "Your brother will rise again". Martha answered, "I know he will rise again in the resurrection at the last day (Day).", (Verses 23&24).

All of this foreshadows that last Day and the emotions of that moment when Jesus calls each of us, by name, out of the grave. What a celebration that will be. This is why it is so important to Jesus that His followers, like Martha, live focused "on that Day" and the celebration that will be sure to follow. And just like what we do today as we celebrate the life of those who have passed on and what they meant to us; Jesus will celebrate and share with them and everybody on that Day, what they meant to Him.

Looking forward, we can all imagine what that Day will be like. It is truly a gift to each of us that John left out the details of that celebration so that we can anticipate and imagine the joy of that future event - that great getting-up morning. The two most important celebrations in the Church today, Christmas and Easter, have become the most unholy of events. What if the Church shifted focus from Jesus's First Advent to The Second Coming? At Christmas and Easter, the holiness and purity that Jesus requires of us would and should replace the obsessive behavior now enjoyed by a world oblivious to the importance of that coming event.

Associating Christmas and Easter with The Second Coming would have a purifying effect on the entire culture. It would also eliminate the practice of putting off the conversion experience until later or to the end of one's life. The purposeful "Death-bed-confession" would be seen as folly having missed a life lived in anticipation and preparation for that great celebration. Those who have been misled will be called out of the grave and witness the merging of Heaven and Earth, the restoration of Paradise and then be banished forever from the New Heaven and New Earth.

Jesus states very clearly that He did not come to condemn the world but to save it - and that an unbelieving world is condemned by its unbelief. It is also very clear that He is coming back as the Righteous Judge, to judge the believing world. He will judge whether the believing world was conquered by the law of love or not. The First Century Christians were conquered by this law of love. The question for Twenty-First Century Christians is Have we been conquered by the law of love?

THE LAST WORD

The idea of shifting the focus of The Christian Culture from Jesus's first advent to The Second Coming has prompted me to think of the feast that Jesus describes at His return. In Matthew 8, soon after the Sermon on the Mount, Jesus is impressed with the faith of the Centurion and says this, starting at verse 10, "...I tell you the truth, I have not found anyone in Israel with such great faith. I say to you that many will come from the east and the west and will take their places at the feast with Abraham, Isaac and Jacob in the kingdom of heaven.".

Just reading to this point, it seems that Jesus will, not only come back for His Church, He will come back for His people also. Jews who have acknowledged that they missed Jesus at His first advent, but that they are not going to miss His Second Coming. This seems to say that the God of second chances is going to give the entire world a second chance to believe in Him and commit to Him in anticipation of His Second Coming. This new focus would have the effect of uniting all people who have Father Abraham and the God of Abraham in common.

The Body of Christ - The Bride of Christ - His Church would be expanded to include all people of The Faith in His return. All those who believe in The God of Abraham but may have been turned off by organized religion or leaders who, for many wrong reasons, have used and abused man's desire to know this God, to serve Him and live in his Kingdom forever.

The common belief of this group of people will be that grace is in The Promise and that faith in The Promise of resurrection would justify them and be counted as righteousness. This defines The Faith of those First-Century Christians and all who pattern their faith after Paul's faith and live in anticipation and preparation of The Second Coming. This group of people will resist the promise of instant salvation and instant heaven coming from the predestination crowd and not be seduced by their offers of easy believism and cheap grace.

The writer of Hebrews allows the possibility that Abraham actually did slay Isaac and that God brought him back to life. In a similar way Peter, in 1Peter 3:19-20 says that Jesus, after death, descended in to hades to preach to sinners of old which leaves the possibility that nothing is final until Final Judgment. This is not something to be preached to the living as another chance. It is there to give comfort to the living who pray for the salvation of loved ones who have passed on without The Faith of those First-Century Christians.

This possibility in Abraham's life would explain the strength of his faith in The Promise. In Peter's letter, what benefit is it for Jesus to preach in hades if not to bring the departed into the saving knowledge of Himself?

Jesus says this in verse 12, "But the subjects of the kingdom will be thrown outside, into the darkness, where there will be weeping and gnashing of teeth." These subjects were Jews, in contrast to those who came from the east and the west. These Jews had God's promise of eternal life, but they needed the faith of those who were witnessing this event. They were being taught to put their hope and faith in The Promise and of being present at this coming event.

The Faith of Paul and those First-Century Christians (Disciples) in this coming event was a prerequisite to receiving what was promised regardless of their ethnicity. Here and elsewhere in Scripture, this sorrowful and angry group of followers are part of the "I never knew you crowd" (evil doers) that Jesus has just identified at the end of The Sermom on the Mount. This passage from Matthew 7:21 to Matthew 8:12 should be read together as a warning to all those who's faith is in the person of Jesus rather than His promise to return, bringing salvation with Him.

God's Grace is in The Promise - Our Faith is in The Promise.

Jesus replied, "No one who puts his hand to the plow and looks back is fit for service in the kingdom of God." Luke 9:62.

"Paul, a servant of God and an apostle of Jesus Christ for the faith of God's elect and the knowledge of the truth that leads to godliness - a faith and knowledge resting on the hope of eternal life, which God, who does not lie, promised before the beginning of time." The first two verses from Paul's letter to Titus. From the NIV prior to 1968.

The following prayer is taken from the "Walk to Emmaus" hand book published by The Upper Room.

Merciful God, we confess that we have not loved you with our whole heart. We have failed to be an obedient church. We have not done your will. We have broken your law. We have rebelled against your love. We have not loved our neighbors, and we have not heard the cry of the needy, forgive us, we pray. Free us for joyful obedience, through Jesus Christ our Lord. Amen.

ABOUT THE AUTHOR

Thomas Fitzhugh Sheets is a seventy-six-year-old semi-retired businessman who, while never attending college, has had a reasonably successful career. He is now living at Providence Farm in Bedford County, Virginia, and presently has a beef cattle operation, raising calves for the feeder market.

During discussions with a friend, a retired pastor, and a marine chaplain who has decided that he is "done with the church," Tom was challenged to write a book. His friend understood his ongoing frustration with both the message and direction of the established church and felt that many others shared this frustration.

Tom, who has a heart for the lost within the church, believes that the church has been hijacked by the instant-gratification crowd. Thus, he felt that he was challenged to address this issue, and as a result of this challenge, The Road to Restoration, The Death of the Promise, and the Resurrection of The Promised were developed.

Lightning Source UK Ltd.
Milton Keynes UK
UKHW021832160123
415467UK00005B/215

9 781959 761396